QUALITY VEGETABLES AND HUMAN HEALTH

QUALITY VEGETABLES AND HUMAN HEALTH

BY

IMRAAN KHAN
ZAHOOR ALI

KNOWLEDGE
BAKERS

KNOWLEDGE BAKERS

ISBN: 9789390013579 (HB)

Published by : **Knowledge Bakers**
Pune, India
Email: knowledgebakers2019@gmail.com

Digitally Printed at : **Replika Press Pvt. Ltd.**

PREFACE

This book mainly focuses on the nutritional quality of vegetables and disease prevention, their production methods, preparation, and cooking methods. It provides useful and interesting information on the nutritional qualities of different vegetables and their roles in disease prevention. Quality vegetable production through hydroponic cultivation techniques is also included. It focuses on the importance of quality vegetables to human diet and health, and non-communicable disease prevention and nutritional qualities and bioactive compounds in freshly grown vegetables through hydroponics and soilless cultures are also discussed. The book serves as a valuable reference book for a variety of readers with an interest in health, nutrition, agriculture, and food science, Farmers and agricultural professionals, nutritionists and dieticians, public health professionals, researchers and general public.

We are grateful to all those persons as well as various books, manuals, periodicals, magazines, journals etc. that helped in the preparation of this book. In spite of the best efforts, it is possible that some errors may have occurred into the compilation and editing of the book. Further queries, constructive suggestions and criticisms for the improvement of the book are always welcomed and shall be thankfully acknowledged.

Imraan Khan
Zahoor Ali

CONTENTS

Chapter 1

Introductory Chapter: Quality Vegetable Production and Human Health Benefits

1. Introduction

Vegetables are the important sources of vitamins, minerals, and antioxidants providing human health benefits. Regular intake of recommended amount of vegetables leads to sound health. On the contrary, insufficient intake of quality vegetables causes several mineral deficiency disease symptoms. Quality of vegetables greatly depends on the production system and handling procedures after harvest. In this case, hydroponic systems are now popularly used for producing quality vegetables. In these managed culture techniques, plants are grown in water or soilless substrates through artificial supply of plant nutrition. In this chapter, the importance of quality vegetables to human health will be discussed. Use of hydroponic systems and soilless culture techniques for the production of quality vegetables will also be discussed briefly.

2. Human health benefits of quality vegetables

The fresh and edible portions of herbaceous plants are generally termed as vegetables, which are important component of a healthy diet. They are the important source of vitamins and minerals, dietary fibers, and antioxidants. Regular and adequate intake of different kinds of vegetables such as edible roots, stems, leaves, fruits, or seeds helps us maintain good health. On the other hand, reduced consumption of quality vegetables often causes noncommunicable diseases including cardiovascular diseases and certain types of cancer. It is estimated that about 5.2 million deaths reported worldwide were due to inadequate consumption of fruits and vegetables in 2013 [1–3]. Research results recommended increased consumption of fruits and vegetables for the prevention of these chronic diseases [4, 5]. Vegetables contain low fats, less sugars, and sodium ions, which are the main focus of healthy diets. In this regards, WHO recommended consumption of more than 400 grams of fruits and vegetables per day to maintain good health and also reduce the risk of noncommunicable diseases [6].

Vegetables provide mineral nutrients that are vital for good health and maintenance of our body. Most of the vegetables have low fat and calories, many mineral nutrients including potassium, dietary fiber, folic acid, vitamin A, and vitamin C. Dietary potassium may help to maintain healthy blood pressure. In this case, vegetables such as sweet potatoes, white potatoes, white beans, tomato products, beet greens, soybeans, lima beans, spinach, lentils, and kidney beans are rich in potassium. Dietary fiber from vegetables helps to reduce blood cholesterol levels and to lower risk of cardiovascular disease. Vegetables containing vitamin A keeps eyes and skin healthy and helps to protect against infections, while vitamin C helps heal cuts and wounds and keeps teeth and gums healthy and it aids in iron absorption.

Vegetable rich diets are attributed to overall good health and reduce the risk of cardiovascular diseases including heart attack and stroke [7]. Colored vegetables are reported to play protective roles against certain types of cancer [8, 9]. Dietary fiber from vegetables such as leafy greens reduces the risk of heart diseases, obesity and diabetes mellitus, and metabolic syndromes [10].

In the following chapter, different types of vegetables such as leafy greens, root, bulb and tubers, legumes, stalks, fruit and flower vegetables are discussed along with their role on prevention of diabetes, obesity, metabolic syndrome, cardiovascular disease, and cancer. Preparation and cooking methods greatly affect the nutritional quality of vegetables. Thus, research results on these preparing and cooking methods will be also discussed in another chapter. Health benefits of common fruits and vegetables in the sub-Saharan Africa with their consumption status will be reviewed in one of chapter of this book.

3. Production techniques of quality vegetables

Quality of vegetable greatly depends on the horticultural production systems [11], environmental factors [12], and management practices used [13]. Climatic conditions such as mainly temperature and light intensity have strong influence on the nutritional quality of vegetables. It was reported that, soil type, rootstock used for fruit trees, mulching, irrigation, fertilization, and other cultural practices influence composition and quality attributes of the harvested plant [14]. Hydroponic cultivation technique ensures production of quality vegetables, as in this culture system both plant nutrition and environmental conditions are artificially managed according to the plant need. Growing quality vegetables is easier and safer in hydroponic system compared to conventional soil culture. The great advantages of this system are that plant roots are visible and root zone environment can be easily monitored [15]. In this system of cultivation, yield of vegetable crop can be maximized though efficient use of all resources, and it is believed to be the most intensive form of agricultural enterprises for commercial production of greenhouse vegetables [16–18].

Soilless culture of vegetables uses either inert organic or inorganic substrate through hydroponic nutrient application. This culture technique has also been reported to practice in the greenhouse as an alternative to conventional filed cultivation of many high-value vegetable crops [19–21].

Under these protected cultivation system, weather factors, amount and composition of nutrient solution, and also the growing medium can be managed successfully. Thus, quality of vegetable crops grown through soilless culture improves significantly compared to conventional soil culture [22, 23]. Many other researchers found better taste, uniformity, color, texture, and higher nutritional value in fruits grown in soilless culture than in soil cultivation methods [24–26].

In this book, nutritional quality and bioactive compounds in freshly grown vegetable through hydroponics will be discussed in detail. Moreover, influence of different soilless substrates on the growth, quality, and yield of Slovenian sweet potato cultivar will also be presented. In the sea, there are abundant sources of green algae that can be included in the dietary menu as it is rich in minerals. The final chapter will describe the methods of sea vegetables utilization in the food formulation.

4. Conclusion

Sufficient consumption of quality vegetables can reduce the risk of several noncommunicable diseases such as cardiovascular disease, cancers, diabetes, obesity, and metabolic syndromes. Inclusion of vegetables in the dietary constituents indicates healthy life. Vegetables provides greater amount of dietary fiber, vitamins, minerals, and also phytochemicals or antioxidants. In this regards, hydroponics and soilless culture can produce higher quality of vegetables compared to traditional soil culture techniques. It is evident that, nutrition-related health problems are increasing drastically in the world. Therefore, production of quality vegetables and their sufficient consumption should be given priority for human health promotion.

References

[1] Agudo A, Cabrera L, Amiano P, Ardanaz E, Barricarte A, Berenguer T, Chirlaue MD, Dorronsora M, Jakszyn P, Larranaga N, Martinez C, Navarro C, Quiros JR, Sanchez MJ, Tormo MJ, Gonzalez CA. Fruit and vegetable intakes, dietary antioxidant nutrients, and total mortality in Spanish adults: Findings from the Spanish cohort of the European prospective investigation into cancer and nutrition (EPIC-Spain). American Journal of Clinical Nutrition 2007;**85**:1634-1642. https://doi.org/10.1093/ajcn/85.6.1634

[2] Nicklett EJ, Semba RD, Xue QL, Tian J, Sun K, Cappola AR, Simonsick EM, Ferrucci L, Fried LP. Fruit and vegetable intake, physical activity, and mortality in older community dwelling women. Journal of the American Geriatrics Society. 2012;**60**:862-868. DOI: 10.1111/j.1532-5415.2012.03924.x

[3] Trichopoulou A, Costacou T, Bamia C, Trichopoulos D. Adherence to a Mediterranean diet and survival in a Greek population. The New England Journal of Medicine. 2003;**348**:2599-2608. DOI: 10.1056/NEJMoa025039

[4] Joint WHO/FAO Expert Consultation. Diet, nutrition and the prevention of chronic diseases. World Health Organization Technical Report Series. 2003;**916**:1-149. http://apps.who.int/iris/bitstream/handle/10665/42665/WHO_TRS_916.pdf;jsessionid=E6EF8E5152 10243920680C81AA3BBF0B?sequence=1 [Accessed: June 04, 2018]

[5] Committee on Diet and Health, National Research Council. Diet and Health: Implications for Reducing Chronic Disease Risk. Washington, D.C.: National Academy Press; 1989. http://www.nap.edu/catalog/1222.html

[6] http://www.who.int/elena/titles/fruit_vegetables_ncds/en/

[7] He FJ, Nowson CA, MacGregor GA. Fruit and vegetable consumption and stroke: Meta-analysis of cohort studies. The Lancet. 2006;**367**:320-326. DOI: 10.1016/S0140-6736 (06)68069-0

[8] Hung HC, Joshipura KJ, Jiang R, Hu FB, Hunter D, Smith-Warner SA, Colditz GA, Rosner B, Spiegelman D, Willett WC. Fruit and vegetable intake and risk of major chronic disease. Journal of the National Cancer Institute. 2004;**96**:1577-1584. DOI: 10.1093/jnci/djh296

[9] Wiseman M. The Second World Cancer Research Fund/American Institute for Cancer Research Expert Report. Food, nutrition, physical activity, and the prevention of cancer: A global perspective: Nutrition society and BAPEN medical symposium on 'Nutrition support in cancer therapy'. Proceedings of the Nutrition Society. 2008;**67**:253-256. DOI: 10.1017/S002966510800712X

[10] Mursu J, Virtanen JK, Toumainen TP, Nurmi T, Voutilainen S. Intake of fruit, berries, and vegetables and risk of type 2 diabetes in finnish men: The Kuopio Ischaemic heart disease risk factor study. The American Journal of Clinical Nutrition. 2014;**99**:328-333. DOI: 10.3945/ajcn.113.069641

[11] Hoagland L, Ximenes E, Ku S, Ladisch M. Foodborne pathogens in horticultural production systems: Ecology and mitigation. Scientia Horticulturae. 2018;**236**:192-206. DOI: 10.1016/j.scienta.2018.03.040

[12] Edelstein M, Ben-Hur M. Heavy metals and metalloids: Sources, risks and strategies to reduce their accumulation in horticultural crops. Scientia Horticulturae. 2018;**234**:431-444. DOI: 10.1016/j.scienta.2017.12.039

[13] Rouphael Y, Kyriacou MC, Petropoulos SA, De Pascale S, Colla G. Improving vegetable quality in controlled environments. Scientia Horticulturae. 2018;**234**:275-289. DOI: 10.1016/j.scienta.2018.02.033

[14] Goldman IL, Kader AA, Heintz C. Influence of production, handling, and storage on phytonutrient content of foods. Nutrition Reviews. 1999;**57**:S46-S52

[15] Hershey DR. Solution culture hydroponics: History & inexpensive equipment. The American Biology Teacher. 1994;**56**:111-118. Available from: http://www.jstor.org/stable/4449764

[16] Dorais M, Papadopoulos AP, Gosselin A. Greenhouse tomato fruit quality. In: Janick J, editor. Horticultural Reviews. Vol. 26. 2001. pp. 239-319. DOI: 10.1002/9780470650806.ch5

[17] Grillas S, Lucas M, Bardopoulou E, Sarafopoulos S, Voulgari M. Perlite based soilless culture systems: Current commercial applications and prospects. Acta Horticulturae. 2001;**548**:105-114. DOI: 10.17660/ActaHortic.2001.548.10

[18] Jensen MH. Food production in greenhouses. In: Goto E, Kurata K, Hayashi M, Sase S, editors. Plant Production in Closed Ecosystems: The International Symposium on Plant Production in Closed Ecosystems held in Narita, Japan; Netherlands: Springer. 26-29 August 1996. pp. 1-14. DOI: 10.1007/978-94-015-8889-8

[19] Blank C. Specialty Process for Specialty Products. Guelph, ON: The Grower; March 1999. p. 28-30

[20] Cantliffe DJ, Shaw NL, Jovicich E, Rodriguez JC, Secker I, Karchi Z. Passive ventilated high-roof greenhouse production of vegetables in a humid, mild winter climate. Acta Horticulturae. 2001;**559**:195-201

[21] Paradossi A, Malorgio F, Campiotti C, Tognoni F. A comparison between two methods to control nutrient delivery to greenhouse melons grown in recirculating nutrient solution culture. Scientia Horticulturae. 2002;**92**:82-95. DOI: 10.1016/S0304-4238(01)00292-8

[22] Xu HL, Gauthier L, Gosselin A. Effects of fertigation management on growth and photosynthesis of tomato plants grown in peat, rockwool and NFT. Scientia Horticulturae. 1995;**6**:11-20. DOI: 10.1016/0304-4238(95)00791-Q

[23] Massantini F, Favilli R, Magnani G, Oggiano N. Soilless culture-biotechnology for high quality vegetables. Soilless Culture. 1988;**4**:27-40

[24] Varis S, Altay H. The most suitable and new method for soilless growing in Turkey: Perlite culture. In: First Perlite Symposium Turkish Agriculture, Izmir, Turkey; 1992. p. 185

[25] Abak K, Celikel G. Comparison of some Turkish originated organic and inorganic substrates for tomato soilless culture. Acta Horticulturae. 1994;**366**:423-427. DOI: 10.17660/ActaHortic.1994.366.52

[26] Alan RA, Zulkadir A, Padem H. The influence of growing media on growth, yield and quality of tomato grown under greenhouse conditions. Acta Horticulturae. 1994;**366**:429-436. DOI: 10.17660/ActaHortic.1994.366.53

Chapter 2

Role of Vegetables in Human Nutrition and Disease Prevention

Abstract

Vegetables are important for human health because of their vitamins, minerals, phytochemical compounds, and dietary fiber content. Especially antioxidant vitamins (vitamin A, vitamin C, and vitamin E) and dietary fiber content have important roles in human health. Adequate vegetable consumption can be protective some chronic diseases such as diabetes, cancer, obesity, metabolic syndrome, cardiovascular diseases, as well as improve risk factors related with these diseases. In this chapter, basic information will be given about the classification of vegetables, preparation and cooking, and their effects on food content of vegetables and effects on health and diseases (diabetes, obesity, metabolic syndrome, cardiovascular diseases, and cancer).

Keywords: vegetables, diabetes, metabolic syndrome, cardiovascular diseases, cancer, cooking methods, phenolic compounds, antioxidants, fiber

1. Introduction

Vegetables are annual or perennial horticultural crops, with certain sections (roots, stalks, flowers, fruits, leaves, etc.) that can be consumed wholly or partially, cooked or raw [1].

Vegetables are important for human nutrition in terms of bioactive nutrient molecules such as dietary fiber, vitamins and minerals, and non-nutritive phytochemicals (phenolic compounds, flavonoids, bioactive peptides, etc.). These nutrient and non-nutrient molecules reduce the risk of chronic diseases such as cardiovascular diseases, diabetes, certain cancers, and obesity [2, 3].

In recent years, consumers began to change their eating patterns with the growing interest in the effect of foods in staying healthy and maintaining health. "Western" type diets are characterized by increased intake of calories, sugar, saturated fats and animal protein, and reduced consumption of vegetables and fruits. When this type of diet is combined with lack of activity, the prevalence and frequency of diseases such as obesity, diabetes, and cardiovascular pathologies also increases [3]. In healthy diets (Mediterranean diet model), eating plant-based foods such as fruits and vegetables, cereals, legumes and nuts, replacing butter with healthy oils such as olive oil and canola oil, using herbs and spices to add flavor instead of salt, limiting red meat to several times a month and eating fish and poultry at least twice a week are recommended. Evidence from epidemiological studies and clinical trials shows that the Mediterranean diet is associated with many positive health outcomes such as reduced risk of various chronic illnesses, reduced overall mortality, and increased likelihood of healthy aging[4].One of the most important features of these diets is the high consumption of vegetables, and therefore fiber, vitamins, minerals, flavonoids, phytoestrogens, sulfur compounds, phenolic compounds such as monoterpenes and bioactive peptides, which have positive effects on health [3]. In this chapter, basic information will be presented on the classification of vegetables, their relation to health, and the effects of preparation and cooking on nutrient content of vegetables.

2. Classification of vegetables

There are approximately 10,000 plant species used as vegetables in the world. Classification of these species can be done by considering a common set of features. It is important for food researchers, dietitians, and nutrition educators to subcategorize vegetables by taking into account health and nutrition. This sub-categorization will be more useful if it is based on similarities in food composition [5]. Vegetables can be classified according to the part of the plant used for nutrition and the specific nutritional value [6].

2.1. Green vegetables

2.1.1. Leaf vegetables

This group includes spinach, lettuce, curly lettuce, chard, purslane, chicory, etc. These are important minerals (iron and calcium), vitamins (A, C, and riboflavin) and fiber sources.

Young, fresh leaves contain more vitamin C than mature plants. The green outer leaves of lettuce and cabbage are richer in vitamins, calcium, and iron than white inner leaves. Thinner and greener leaves are more nutritious and usually have lower calories.

2.1.2. Stalk vegetables

The best examples to be given to stalk vegetables are celery and asparagus. They contain minerals and vitamins in proportion to the green color. Asparagus is a particularly rich source of folic acid.

2.1.3. *Fruit and flower vegetables*

Broccoli, cauliflower, and artichoke are frequently consumed flowering vegetables. Broccoli is a good source of iron, phosphorus, vitamins A and C, and riboflavin. Cauliflower is also a good source of vitamin C. The nutritional value of the outer leaves of cauliflower and broccoli is much higher than the flower buds. They can be consumed raw in salads or cooked. Artichoke is a good source of minerals, especially potassium, calcium, and phosphorus, and has high dietary fiber content. Tomatoes and peppers are the most common fruit vegetables. Both are rich in vitamin C. Other fruit vegetables include cucumber, zucchini, and eggplant. A dark green or yellow color indicates high β-carotene content. The darker the yellow color, the higher the content of β-carotene.

2.2. Root vegetables

2.2.1. *Root, bulb, and tuber vegetables*

Carrot, beet, turnip, fennel, onion, radish, and potato are examples of this group of vegetables. Yellow and orange varieties are rich in β-carotene, which is the precursor of vitamin A. Onion is an extraordinary example of root vegetables and contains moderate levels of vitamin C.

2.2.2. *Legumes*

This group includes legumes, peas, and soya beans. This group is rich in saponin and soluble fiber [6].

Subgroups may differ from country to country and classifications in nutritional guidelines are based on nutritional content in different countries. For example, the basic food guidelines used in the United States (Basic 7 and Basic 4 Food Groups and Food Guide Pyramid) are focused on dark green leafy and dark orange/yellow group vegetables for beta-carotene and citrus fruits for vitamin C. Later on, 2010 USDA MyPyramid food guide identified dark green leafy vegetables and broccoli, other leafy vegetables, legumes, unique vegetables (dark orange, tomato, allium vegetables, etc.) and additional vegetables [**Table 1**]. In the guide prepared by Turkish Ministry of Health (Turkey Nutrition Guide 2015), vegetables have been classified as *Dark green leafy vegetables* (Mediterranean/salad greens such as spinach, chard, quince, blackcurrant, vine leaf, curly, lettuce, spinach, purslane, parsley, cress, arugula, mint, sorrel, radish, dill, radica, and curly-chicory (chopped or in salads)), *other green vegetables* (broccoli, okra, fresh beans, fresh peas, green zucchini, artichokes, asparagus, brussels sprouts, varieties of pointed or stuffed peppers, cucumber, and iceberg lettuce (chopped or in salads)), *Red—orange—blue—purple vegetables* (tomatoes, carrots, red pepper, radish, winter squash, beet, aubergine, and red cabbage), *white vegetables* (onion, celery, cabbage, cauliflower, leek, mushroom, ground apple, turnip), and *starchy vegetables* (potatoes and fresh corn) [7].

Vegetable subgroups	Important sources[a]	Contributes[b]
Dark green leafy vegetables and broccoli	Vitamin C	Iron, copper, manganese
	Vitamin K	Vitamin B6
	Folate	Phytosterol
	Beta-carotene	Alpha-carotene
	Lutein + zeaxanthin, flavones	Flavonols
		TAC
Other leafy vegetables	Vitamin C	Phytosterol
	Vitamin K	Manganese
	Anthocyanidins	Vitamin B6
		Folate
		Beta-carotene
		Lutein + zeaxanthin
		TAC
Legumes	Copper	Dietary fiber
	Folate	Magnesium, iron, zinc, manganese
	Phytosterol	Vitamin B6
	Flavan-3-ols	
	Flavonols	
	TAC	
Unique vegetables	Vitamin C	Vitamin B6
	Alpha-carotene lycopene	Vitamin K
		Manganese, copper
		Beta-carotene
Additional vegetables	Flavonoids	Vitamin C
		Vitamin K

[a]Provides >25% DRI or highest mean concentration of component per 100 g.
[b]Provides >10% DRI or second or third highest concentration of component per 100 g.

Table 1. Summary chart for food ingredients in 2010 my pyramid vegetable subgroups [5].

3. The effect of vegetables on some disease

3.1. Effects on diabetes, obesity, and metabolic syndrome

Diabetes mellitus (DM), obesity, and the metabolic syndrome (MS) are increasing health problems in recent years in parallel with the increase in unhealthy eating habits and unhealthy living behaviors. One of the most basic aspects of the control and management of the disease in individuals with these health problems is the regulation of eating habits. In medical nutrition therapy applied to these individuals, it is important to meet the energy and nutritional needs of individuals, as well as including foods with functional activities against the complications of these diseases in the diet. Phytochemical compounds (carotenoids, alkaloids, terpenoids, and phenolics), which are secondary compounds found in vegetables, are thought to be protective against these diseases.

3.1.1. *Root, bulb, and tuber vegetables*

Onions and garlic, thanks to the volatile oils, organosulfur compounds, and flavonoids in their content, are among the vegetables thought to be protective against DM, obesity, and MS [8]. Organosulfur compounds such as S-methyl cysteine and flavonoids such as quercetin in these vegetables exert a functional effect by regulating the activities of some enzymes involved in carbohydrate metabolism, increasing insulin secretion and sensitivity, and increasing NADP+ and NADPH activities [9]. In addition, these vegetables inhibit the enzymes α-glucosidase and α-amylase, inhibiting the formation of D-glucose from oligosaccharides and disaccharides and delaying the absorption of glucose from the intestines [10]. Onion and garlic are especially protective against dyslipidemia and oxidative stress, which are seen due to DM and MS.

Kumar et al. found that obese patients with Type 2 diabetes who used garlic tablets in addition to metformin had significantly higher fasting blood glucose (FBG), postprandial blood glucose, total cholesterol (TC), triglyceride (TG), low density lipoprotein cholesterol (LDL), C-reactive protein (CRP), and adenosine deaminase levels compared to those of patients using only metformin [11]. In dyslipidemic individuals with Type 2 DM, the use of garlic tablets for 12 weeks significantly decreased TC and LDL levels, while high-density lipoprotein cholesterol (HDL) levels were significantly increased [12]. Although there are similar studies suggesting that garlic has positive effects on blood glucose level and plasma lipid profile in the presence of DM [13], garlic was also found to increase antioxidant enzyme activities in DM and reduce bioactive aldehyde levels [14].

It was found that garlic consumption increased adiponectin levels in MS patients [15]. Considering that adiponectin has antiatherogenic and antiatherosclerotic effects [16], garlic consumption in MS patients is thought to be protective against cardiovascular diseases (CVDs). In addition, it has been determined that garlic has a positive effect on insulin resistance in rats with MS induced by high fructose content feed [17].

In obese rats induced by high-fat diets, garlic supplemented animal feed reduced TG and TC levels, as well as body weight and epididymal fat accumulation [18]. Similarly, in obesity induced rats with a high-fat diet, garlic reduced visceral and epididymal fat accumulation while reducing atherogenic index and cardiac risk factors [19].

It was reported that onion powder added to animal feed in experimental diabetic rats induced by aloxane or streptozotocin had a hypoglycemic effect [9, 20]. In a study comparing the efficacy of glibenclamide, which is an oral antidiabetic drug, with onion application at different doses in DM rats, it was reported that 300 mg/kg of onion extract application reduced fasting glucose levels by 75.4%, whereas 2.5 mg/kg glibenclamide reduced fasting glucose levels by 76.4% [21].

Studies investigating the effects of onion consumption in the presence of DM on antioxidant enzyme levels such as superoxide dismutase (SOD), catalase (CAT), and glutathione peroxidase (GSH-Px) showed that onion consumption increased the levels of these enzymes [22]. In these studies, it was also found that onion reduced bioactive aldehyde levels such as malondialdehyde (MDA) formed by the decomposition of lipid hydroperoxides.

It was reported that onion reduced insulin resistance and improved FBG levels in MS Zucker type rats [23]. It was shown that onion extract reduced weight gain, epididymal fat accumulation, and serum TC levels in BALB/c mice that were made obese with a high-fat diet [24]. It was reported that a daily onion consumption of 100–120 g significantly decreased TC and LDL cholesterol levels of obese women with polycystic ovary syndrome [25].

3.1.2. Leaf vegetables

Purslane and chard are green leafy vegetables thought to have functional activity against DM, MS, and obesity. Purslane shows a functional effect due to free oxalic acids, alkaloids, omega-3 fatty acids, coumarins, flavonoids, cardiac glycosides, anthraquinone, α-linolenic acid, and active compounds in its composition [26], while chard shows its effect via phospholipids, glycolipids, fatty acids (palmitic, stearic, oleic, and linoleic acid), folic acid, ascorbic acid, and pectin in its composition [27]. Purslane, described by WHO as one of the most used medical plants, is also called "global panacea" [28].

In studies investigating the effects of the use of purslane extract on anthropometric and biochemical changes in Type 2 DM patients, it was found that consumption of purslane extract significantly reduced HbA1c levels [29], TG, TC, LDL, FBG, and post-prandial blood glucose, body weight and BMI, whereas it significantly increased HDL levels [30]. In another study, consumption of purslane extract significantly increased glucagon-like peptide-1 concentrations, which has positive effects on beta cell proliferation and insulin secretion, in individuals with Type 2 DM [31].

In rats fed high-fat diets, it was seen that purslane decreased TG, TC, and LDL levels [32] and similarly it decreased TC and TG levels in hypercholesterolemic rats [33]. In rats with DM induced by streptozotocin, it was shown that purslane had hypoglycemic [34] and antioxidant effects [35].

In Type 1 diabetic rats, chard extracts were shown to reduce blood glucose levels and improve beta cell regeneration [27], while significantly decreasing adenosine deaminase levels [36]. It was also found that chard decreased elevated MDA levels due to diabetes and increased antioxidant capacity [36]. In Type 2 diabetic rats, chard extract was also shown to be effective in increasing insulin secretion and lowering blood glucose levels by increasing GLP-1 and acetylcholine levels [37]. It was also found to have a hypolipidemic effect in high fat diet-induced rats [38].

3.1.3. Fruit and flower vegetables

Broccoli and cauliflower are vegetables thought to have protective effects against many diseases thanks to glucosinolates and indole-3-carbinol they contain [39]. Indole-3-carbinol given to obesity induced mice by a high fat diet was shown to reduce epididymal fat accumulation, body weight, insulin, leptin, and blood glucose levels, increase adiponectin levels, and improve glucose tolerance [39]. Similarly, in Type 2 diabetic rats fed with a high fat diet, indole-3-carbinol reduced blood glucose levels, and HbA1c levels, thereby reducing thiobarbituric acid reactive substances, lipid hydroperoxides and conjugated dienes levels, and increased levels of SOD, CAT, and GSH-Px [40]. Positive effects of broccoli on impaired lipid profile due to high fat diets were detected [41].

3.1.4. Legumes

Leguminosae family peas and vegetables such as peas and soybeans inhibit alpha-amylase enzyme, and show antidyslipidemic and antioxidant effects thanks to phytosterols such as B-sitosterol, campesterol and stigmasterol, and linoleic acid they contain [42]. Studies conducted by Helmstädter revealed that different plant extracts of this family improved glucose tolerance and glycosuria [43]. Consumption of different species of this family such as Pinto beans, Great Northern beans, Navy beans, and Black beans have been reported to reduce the risk of obesity, MS, and DM [44].

3.2. Effects on cardiovascular diseases

CVDs are the primary cause of death and illness in the world. The Global Burden of Disease Study reported that 29.6% of all deaths in the world were due to CVDs [45]. The main factor in these deaths is the increase in unhealthy lifestyle and eating habits. Most of the risk factors associated with CVDs are reversible risk factors and non-pharmacologic measures such as healthy eating habits and healthy lifestyle changes may help control the risk factors for the disease. Increased consumption of vegetables, which are an important part of a healthy diet, has been shown to reduce CVD-related mortality rates [46] and improve risk factors [47]. Vegetables are protective against CVD thanks to low content of saturated fat, trans fat, and cholesterol and being rich in bioactive compounds such as flavonoids, phytoestrogens (lignans, coumestran, isoflavones, resveratrol, and lycopene), organosulfur compounds, soluble dietary fibers (β-glucan, pectin, and psyllium), isothiocyanates, monoterpenes, and sterols (sitostanol, stigmasterol, and campesterol) [48].

3.2.1. Root, bulb, and tuber vegetables

Epidemiological studies indicate that there is an inverse relationship between garlic consumption and CVD development. Studies in the literature reported that garlic and garlic components show cholesterol and lipid lowering effects by inhibiting key enzymes involved in cholesterol and fatty acid synthesis (monooxygenase and HMG-CoA reductase) [49], antiplatelet effect by inhibiting cyclooxygenase enzyme activity [50], and fibrinolytic effect by inhibiting lipid peroxidation and hemolysis in oxidized erythrocytes [51]. It was also reported that onion and garlic had a blood pressure lowering effect by inducing intracellular nitric oxide and hydrogen sulfide production and inhibiting angiotensin-converting enzyme activity [52]. It was also shown that garlic reduced the levels of reactive oxygen species (ROS) that are thought to play a role in the pathogenesis of CVD and increased antioxidant capacity [52].

Although epidemiological studies investigating the relationship of onion consumption and CVD risk and CVD-related mortality rates are limited, a study conducted in Finland found that CVD-induced mortality was lower in individuals with high onion consumption than in those with low onion consumption [53]. Similar to garlic, onion also improves cardiovascular health through the sulfurous compounds, and especially flavonoids such as quercetin in its content. By cutting an onion, *S*-alk(en)yl-L-cysteine sulfoxides are converted into thiosulfinates and copaenes via the enzyme alliinase and these compounds inhibit platelet aggregation [54]. Since platelet aggregation is an important risk factor for the development of coronary thrombosis and atherosclerosis, onion consumption may be beneficial in individuals with risk factors for CVD. In addition, it was reported that onion consumption in hypercholesterolemic rats reduces CVD risk by decreasing the elevated inflammatory biomarkers associated with high cholesterol diet and by increasing the levels of antioxidant enzymes [55]. Onion also eliminates risk factors by correcting the dyslipidemia seen in some chronic diseases such as DM [9].

3.2.2. *Leaf vegetables*

Green leafy vegetables increase antioxidant capacity through minerals, vitamins, pulp, and phytochemical compounds in their content and protect against oxidative stress which is thought to play an important role in the pathogenesis of CVD [56]. In traditional diets where consumption of green leafy vegetables is high (Mediterranean and Japanese traditional diets), the rate of CVD is lower, and average life span is longer [57]. Moreover, in vegetarian individuals, mortality rates due to ischemic heart diseases and cerebrovascular diseases were also found to be lower than in non-vegetarians [58]. In another study, it was found that paralysis rates were significantly lower in individuals with higher consumption of green leafy vegetables than in individuals with less consumption of green leafy vegetables [59]. The incidence of coronary artery disease was also reported to be lower in individuals with higher green leafy vegetables consumption [53]. Individuals with more than three portions of green leafy vegetable consumption a day were found to have an ischemic heart disease incidence of about 60% less than those consuming less than 1 portion per day [60]. Furthermore, green leafy vegetables such as rocket, spinach, and lettuce also reduce blood pressure, inhibit platelet aggregation and improve endothelial dysfunction due to their rich inorganic nitrate content [57]. Some studies suggest that high nitrate content in the vegetables in this group is transformed into nitrite, nitric oxide, and vasodilator-tissue protective secondary compounds through symbiotic bacteria in the oral cavity, thereby maintaining cardiopulmonary function by lowering blood pressure [61].

3.2.3. *Fruit and flower vegetables*

The vegetables in this group are rich in sulfur-containing glucosinolates, flavonoids, anthocyanins, coumarins, carotenoids, antioxidant enzymes, and terpenes [62]. However, indole-3-carbinol and sulforaphane, which is a hydrolysis product of glucoraphanin, are thought to be the main bioactive compounds that are protective against CVD [63]. In experimental animals, sulforaphane protects against ischemic damage to the heart through induction of

Nrf2-related phase-II enzymes such as SOD, CAT, and hemoxygenase-1 [64]. Indole-3-carbinol and sulforaphane also protect against inflammation by inhibiting cytokine production [63]. In some epidemiological studies, it has been argued that consumption of vegetables in this group may reduce CVD-related mortality rates [65, 66]. It has been reported that anthocyanins extracted from red cabbage have protective effect on blood platelets [67], while broccoli sprouts decrease TC and LDL levels and increase HDL levels [68].

3.2.4. Legumes

The vegetables in this group are protective against CVD due to their high saponin and soluble fiber content. Another reason why legumes are beneficial for heart health is their low sodium and high potassium, calcium, and magnesium content [69]. The soluble pulp reduces the levels of TC and LDL by inhibiting the absorption of bile acid from the intestines and enabling the formation of short chain fatty acids, particularly propionic acid, that inhibit the synthesis of cholesterol [70]. It also improves heart health by inhibiting platelet aggregation [71]. In long-term observational epidemiologic studies, increased legume consumption has been reported to reduce CVD-related mortality and may protect against these diseases [69, 72, 73].

3.3. Effects on cancer

Cancer occurs as cells grow and proliferative without control [74]. Cancer occurs, progresses, and spreads as a result of abnormal signals in the body due to genetic or epigenetic effects [75]. Cancer is among the main causes of death in the world. On average, 16% of deaths occur each year due to cancer [76]. Lifestyle and many genetic and environmental factors can cause cancer. Smoking, consumed foods, solar radiation, and carcinogens in the environment are among these factors. The most important step in the treatment of cancer is the prevention of cancer. In particular, it is important to use health-related preventive practices in the communities and individuals at risk [75].

Consuming plant-based foods, especially increasing the consumption of vegetables, reduces the risk of cancer [74]. The antioxidants in vegetables help reduce the risk of cancer by preventing oxidative damage to the cells in the body [77]. Vegetables have protective effects against cancer due to the vitamins, minerals, pulp, and phytochemicals they contain [78]. About 14% of deaths worldwide due to inadequate vegetable consumption are caused by gastrointestinal cancers [79].

In a meta-analysis, the effects of vegetable consumption on cancer incidence were examined. Fruit and vegetable consumption were found to decrease cancer risk independently of each other and it was found that an extra portion of vegetables consumed daily resulted in a 3% reduction in cancer incidence [80].

A study investigating the relationship between vegetable and fruit consumption and epithelial ovarian cancer included 500 cancer patients and 500 control subjects. Cancer patients were found to have significantly lower average amounts of vegetables and fruits consumed per day than the control group [81]. However, in a cohort study investigating the relationship between vegetable and fruit consumption and pancreatic cancer, no significant relationship was found [82].

3.3.1. Root, bulb, and tuber vegetables

Vegetables in this group exert their protective effect against cancer through inositol, flavonoids, lignans, polyphenols, protease inhibitors, saponins, steroids, triterpenoids, isoflavones, phenolic acids, protein kinase inhibitors, sphingolipids, allicin, aline, and allyl sulfides [78].

Onions prevent tumor formation and cancer cells from spreading in many kinds of cancers such as stomach, ovary, breast, and colon cancer [83]. It has been shown that onion extract has apoptosis-inducing effects in MDA-MB-231 cells that cause breast cancer [84].

Compounds such as thyroallyl found in garlic are effective in preventing cancer. Such compounds in garlic have antioxidant effects that prevent and reduce carcinogens in DNA. They are also effective in reducing free radicals, inducing apoptosis, and stimulating the immune system [85, 86]. In a meta-analysis, the relationship between all cancer types and garlic consumption was investigated and it was concluded that garlic consumption was protective against gastric and intestinal cancers [87].

A controlled study investigating the relationship between onion and garlic consumption and gastric cancer included 759 cancer patients and 750 control subjects. As a result of the study, both onion and garlic consumption were found to have a negative relationship with cancer [88].

Carrot, which is a good source of flavonoids, polyacetylenes, vitamins and minerals, and carotenes, is also effective in protecting against cancer. Carrots have antioxidant, anticarcinogenic, and immune system enhancing properties [89]. In a study, it was determined that carrot consumption was negatively related to prostate cancer [90]. In another study conducted on rats, carrot consumption was shown to have protective effects against cancer due to the high content of carotenoids found in carrots [91].

3.3.2. Leaf vegetables

Green leafy vegetables reduce the risk of cancer due to phytochemicals, vitamin C, vitamin E, vitamin K, and vitamin A they contain [92]. The phytochemicals in these vegetables strengthen the immune system, protect against carcinogenic substances, reduce inflammation and oxidative stress that causes cancer, reduce DNA damage, prevent the growth of cancer cells, inhibit angiogenesis that is effective in tumor growth and regulate hormones [78, 93]. It is thought that these effects are exerted especially in cancer types such as breast, skin, lung, and stomach [78]. The main phytochemicals believed to be protective against these cancer types are isothiocyanates [92]. Apart from these phytochemicals, green leafy vegetables are protective against cancer, especially gastrointestinal system carcinomas, due to high pulp content [93].

In this group, spinach shows protective effects against cancer by reducing oxidative stress in the body thanks to vitamins A, C, and E, carotenes such as beta carotene and lutein, flavones and flavonoids it contains [94, 95].

Broccoli is another vegetable that is effective in protecting against cancer. A number of epidemiological studies have associated broccoli to low incidence of cancer. Sulfurous compounds found in broccoli are cancer preventive agents [96]. In addition to sulfurous compounds, there are carotenes and other antioxidant vitamins in broccoli. But the most effective compounds in preventing cancer are the sulfurous compounds in broccoli. These sulfurous compounds inhibit cancer formation by reducing free radicals and preventing cell damage [97].

3.3.3. *Fruit and flower vegetables*

Tomato, a good source of beta carotene and lycopene, reduces free radical damage in the DNA that causes cancer and prevents the growth and spread of cancer cells just like green leafy vegetables [78]. Lycopene is especially protective against prostate cancer [78, 98].

In an epidemiological study, consuming tomato and tomato products was found to be associated with a lower incidence of prostate cancer [99].

Results of a study investigating the relationship of tomatoes and tomato products with cancer revealed that the consumption of tomatoes and tomato products decreased cancer risk [98].

In another study, lycopene in tomatoes was shown to inhibit the growth and spread of cancer cells in lung cancer by reducing oxidative stress and inducing apoptosis [100].

Another vegetable in this group associated with cancer is pepper because of the capsaicin it contains. Capsaicin is thought to prevent cancer cells from growing, developing, and spreading [101].

4. Effect of preparing and cooking methods on vegetables

Vegetables are one of the most important components of human diet and are rich sources of β-carotene (provitamin A), thiamine (B1), riboflavin (B2), niacin (B3), pantothenic acid (B5), pyridoxine (B6), folic acid, ascorbic acid (vitamin C), vitamins E and K, minerals (such as iron, zinc, calcium, magnesium, and selenium), antioxidants (such as carotenoids, polyphenols, and glucosinolates), and fiber [102].

Preparation and cooking methods can greatly affect the nutritional content and acceptability of vegetables. There is no consensus in the literature as to what is the best way of preserving bioactive compounds while preparing and cooking vegetables [103].

Some vegetables are subjected to peeling in order to remove their shell or skin and make them more digestible. Minerals and other nutrients are affected by peeling. This can also cause severe loss of certain vitamins. It is known that peeling before boiling increases the loss of ascorbic acid, folic acid, or other vitamins of group B. Chopping vegetables can also change the bioavailability of bioactive compounds such as vitamins, carotenoids, polyphenols, and flavonoids [104].Thawing, cutting, and crashing citrus vegetables can also disrupt antioxidant glucosinolates due to the presence of myrosinase enzyme found in these vegetables [105].

Cooking improves the flavor of vegetables and enables the nutrients in the vegetables to be more easily used by the digestive system. However, cooking results in some physical and chemical changes in vegetables [106]. The effect of cooking procedure may vary depending on the various factors such as cooking technique, temperature, leakage into the cooking environment, solvent used for extraction, surface area exposed to water and oxygen, and pH [107]. In addition, each food matrix contains different compounds; therefore the same cooking technique may have different effects depending on the type of vegetable [108].

The most commonly used cooking methods are steaming, roasting, boiling, frying, sautéing, sous vide, microwave, and pressure cooking [109]. Cooking techniques affect polyphenol content and antioxidant activity levels in vegetables. Heat treatment can lead to a change in the chemical structures of vegetables, leading to the breakdown of cells and the degradation of some phenolic compounds from biological structures, the release of phenolics from the food matrix, and the conversion of insoluble phenolics to more soluble forms [110, 111]. In addition, the phenolic compounds are soluble in water. Thus, water-based cooking techniques often lead to loss of phenolics by leaking [103].

It has been reported that food processing has negative effects due to oxidation dependent losses in carotenoids and positive effects as it provides increased bioavailability [112]. Among the causes of increased carotenoid concentration in heat treatment may be greater extractability, enzymatic breakdowns, and incalculable moisture losses. Heat treatment also causes inactivation of enzymes and degradation of structures in the food matrix leading to increased bioavailability [113, 114].

The losses of minerals during preparation and cooking stages of vegetables are closely related to their solubility. Minerals are generally stable against a large number of conditions encountered during cooking, such as heat, oxidation, acidity or alkalinity. Potassium is an abundant mineral found in vegetables, and because of its high solubility in water, it is easily lost by leakage during cooking. Calcium and magnesium are usually present in an attached form in plant tissue and are therefore not easily lost by leakage. The loss of vitamin C is due in part to oxidative degradation during preparation and cooking and partly due to the leakage of the vitamin into the water used for cooking. The amount of vitamins degraded during cooking may be quite small compared to the amount lost due to leakage [115]. Due to its solubility and reactivity, folate is susceptible to potentially large losses during food processing and storage. The chemical stability of folates in plant-based foods may be adversely affected by heat, oxygen exposure, and light intensity. Since folate is highly soluble, its losses occur by leakage through the water used for washing, boiling, and cooking [116].

4.1. Root, bulb, and tuber vegetables

Onion is the richest source of quercetin, which is a flavonoid, and it is most widely used source in diet. Gennaro et al. found a 21% reduction in total quercetin uptake after onion peeling [117].

In another study on onions, the effects of boiling, microwaving, frying, and warm holding onion at 60°C for 1–2 hours on flavonoid amounts were investigated and peeling and boiling were found to decrease flavonoid levels in onion by up to 50%. It was found that other cooking methods and warming treatments did not have a significant effect on flavonoid amount [118].

Regarding the effects of cooking on onions, Lombard et al. found a 7% increase in flavonol concentration when sautéed, a 25% increase when oven baking, and an 18% decrease when boiled. They also stated that less than 5 minutes of cooking can result in retention of more than 80% of flavonols [119].

Potato contains various phenolic compounds, mainly chlorogenic acid and caffeic acid. There are several studies showing that cooking reduces [120], does not affect [121] or increases [122–125] phenolic compounds in potato. The reason for the increase in phenolic compounds during cooking is attributed to the increase in the extractability of these compounds from the cellular matrix of potato due to the textural changes in its starch structure during cooking [122].

Carrot is one of the important root vegetables rich in bioactive compounds such as carotenoids and dietary fiber. Bembem and Sadana investigated the effects of different cooking methods (boiling, steaming, pressure cooking, microwaving, and sautéing) on total phenolic content (TPC), total flavonoid content (TFC), total carotenoid and β-carotene content and antioxidant activity, and found that sautéing was the method that increased total carotene, β-carotene, and TPC the most. They reached the conclusion that sautéing and microwaving were the most appropriate ways of cooking carrots [126].

When the effect of boiling and steaming of frozen carrot on phenolic compound content was investigated, it was determined that phenolic content of carrot was significantly decreased at the end of the boiling process, whereas there was an increase in the steaming method [127]. The decrease during boiling may be due to the leakage of phenolic compounds into the boiling water.

4.2. Leaf vegetables

In a study investigating the effect of different cooking methods (boiling, steam cooking, and microwave cooking) on phytochemical content and total antioxidant capacity (TAC) of cabbage and black cabbage, which are part of the *Brassicaceae* family and are rich sources of vitamins and phytochemical compounds such as carotenoids and polyphenols, it was found that the best method in preserving the nutritious quality of vegetables was steam cooking. It was also shown that fresh vegetables preserved phytochemical compounds and TAC better than frozen samples [128].

Chang et al. studied the losses in nutritional value of several green leafy vegetables including Chinese cabbage (*Brassica pekinensis* var. *Cephalata*), swamp cabbage (*Ipomoea aquatica*), spinach (*Spinacia oleracea*), Ceylon spinach (*Basella rubra*), red spinach (*Amaranthus gangeticus*), white spinach (*Amaranthus viridis*), and Tapioca sprouts (*Manihot utilissima*) when they were treated with boiling or deep frying for 4 and 8 minutes, and found that frying reduced lutein content in all vegetables by 8–89%, and boiling reduced lutein content by 0–428%. When 8 minutes boiling procedure was compared with the 4 minutes procedure, β-carotene retention in vegetables other than Chinese cabbage and spinach changed between 18 and 380%, whereas in the frying procedure β-carotene retention increased by 2–3 times except spinach [129]. The difference in cooking conditions (time and temperature), the type of vegetables, and the interaction between cooking methods and vegetable type may be the cause of differences observed in carotenoid composition.

4.2.1. *Fruit and flower vegetables*

Alvi et al. investigated the effects of peeling on tomato, which contains vitamins A, C, and E, as well as various phytochemical compounds including lycopene, and found a reduction of 18.3% in fiber, 25.4% in calcium, 32.6% in magnesium, 6.4% in phosphor, 2.9% in potassium, 28.9% in ascorbic acid, and 17.2% in folic acid after peeling [130].

Dolinsky et al. found that the cooking method that maximized the polyphenol concentration and antioxidant capacity of tomatoes was steaming, and that microwaving significantly reduced the polyphenol content in tomatoes, and recommended microwave cooking less than other cooking methods (boiling, steaming, and pressure cooking) [131].

Pepper (*Capsicum annuum* L.) is considered to be an excellent source of antioxidants and is very rich in ascorbic acid and other phytochemicals. In a study conducted with six species of pepper, three different cooking methods were used (frying, boiling, and microwaving) and antioxidant properties of peppers after cooking procedures were evaluated. Reductions in radical scavenging activity (RSA) and total phenolic contents (TP) were observed after all cooking procedures, but the reductions after frying and microwaving were not statistically significant when compared to the initial RSA and TP levels. After a 5-minutes boiling, a 77% reduction compared to initial RSA levels was obtained, and when the boiling time increased to 30 minutes, the RSA totals decreased significantly compared to raw peppers. Significant reductions were also observed in TP after 5 and 30 minutes of boiling [132]. Based on these results, it can be said that the most suitable heat treatment method for peppers are microwave use and frying. If boiling is to be performed, shorter cooking time, less water usage, and consumption of cooking water can also reduce the amount of antioxidants that can be lost.

Artichoke, which is characterized by a complex antioxidant profile, contains many bioactive compounds such as glycosides and phenolic compounds, especially caffeicinic acid. Ferracane et al. applied boiling, frying, and steam cooking methods on artichoke and found an increase in overall caffeicinic acid concentration due to the formation of different dicaffeicinic acid isomers in cooked artichokes compared to raw ones. However, a higher increase in the concentration of dicaffeicinic acid was observed in steamed and fried artichokes compared to those boiled. In addition, flavonoid concentrations were reduced in all cooking processes and this reduction was largest in frying [133].

In a study comparing vitamin C content of raw, boiled, and microwaved broccoli and cauliflower, significant reductions in vitamin C contents were found after cooking processes. Boiling process caused more vitamin C loss compared to microwaving. After 6 minutes of boiling, vitamin C levels decreased by 64.5% in broccoli, by 70.7% in white cabbage, and by 66.8% in cauliflower [134]. Based on the results, it can be said that microwaving may be preferred instead of boiling to reduce vitamin C losses.

Yuan et al. investigated the effects of steaming, microwaving, boiling, frying, and boiling followed by frying processes on vitamin C levels in broccoli. At the end of the study, it was found that in all procedures except the steaming method, loss of vitamin C was significant compared to initial levels and the highest loss was obtained in boiling followed by frying (38%) and boiling (33%) [135].

When we look at other studies conducted with broccoli belonging to the *Brassicaceae* family, it is also seen that steaming is the best way to preserve nutritional quality of broccoli [107, 136–138].

It is known for a long time that loss of nutrients in vegetables occurs during the preparation and cooking stages. Knowing the conditions that cause these losses can help limit the losses and increase the nutritional quality of the foods.

5. Conclusion

Numerous preclinical studies carried out in recent years have identified beneficial protective and enhancing effects of vegetables on health, resulting from the nutritional and non-nutritional phytochemical contents of vegetables. These phytochemicals have the ability to modify the cellular function by modulating transcription factors and altering gene expression, cellular metabolism, and cellular signaling. The World Health Organization (WHO) recommends daily intake of 5–8 portions (400–600 g) of fruits and vegetables to reduce the risk of micro nutrient deficiency, cardiovascular diseases, cancer, cognitive impairment, and other nutritional health risks.

In order to make optimum use of the nutritional content of vegetables, choosing the right methods of preparation and cooking is as important as the consumption of adequate amounts of vegetables. To minimize nutritional losses, vegetables should be chopped right before cooking, if possible by hand or by metal tools while making the minimum contact possible, each vegetable should be cooked with the method and time that is most appropriate for that vegetable, and consumed as soon as possible.

Conflict of interest

There is no 'conflict of interest'.

References

[1] Welbaum GE. Vegetable production and practices; IARC handbooks of cancer prevention: Fruit and vegetables. In: Vegetable History, Nomenclature, and Classification. 2015;**8**: 1-15

[2] Pennington JAT, Fisher RA. Classification of fruits and vegetables. Journal of Food Composition and Analysis. 2009;**22**(1):23-31

[3] Septembre-Malaterreb A, Remizeb F, Pouchereta P. Fruits and vegetables, as a source of nutritional compounds and phytochemicals: Changes in bioactive compounds during lactic fermentation. Food Research International. 2018;**104**:86-99

[4] Tuttolomondo A, Casuccio A, Butta C, Pecoraro R, Di Raimondo D, Della Corte V, Arnao V, Clemente G, Maida C, Simonetta I, Miceli G, Lucifora B, Cirrincione A, Di Bona D, Corpora F, Maugeri R, Iacopino DG, Pinto A. Mediterranean diet in patients with acute ischemic stroke: Relationships between Mediterranean diet score, diagnostic subtype, and stroke severity index. Atherosclerosis. 2015;**243**:260-267

[5] Pennington JAT, Fisher RA. Food component profiles for fruit and vegetable subgroups. Journal of Food Composition and Analysis. 2010;**23**:411-418

[6] Lintas C. Nutritional aspects of fruit and vegetable consumption. In: Lauret F, editor. Les fruits et légumes dans les économies méditerranéennes: actes du colloque de Chania. Montpellier: CIHEAM; 1992. pp. 79-87

[7] Sağlık, Bakanlığı T.C. Türkiye Beslenme Rehberi 2015. T.C. Sağlık Bakanlığı. TÜRKİYE. Yayın No: 1031. 2016. p. 288

[8] Belemkar S, Dhameliya K, Pata MK. Comparative study of garlic species (*Allium sativum* and *Allium porrum*) on glucose uptake in diabetic rats. Journal of Taibah University Medical Sciences. 2013;**8**:80-85. DOI: 10.1016/j.jtumed.2013.04.002

[9] Akash MSH, Rehman K, Chen S. Spice plant *Allium cepa*: Dietary supplement for treatment of type 2 diabetes mellitus. Nutrition. 2014;**30**:1128-1137. DOI: 10.1016/j.nut.2014.02.011

[10] Nickavar B, Yousefian N. Inhibitory effects of six allium species on-amylase enzyme activity. Iranian Journal of Pharmaceutical Research. 2010;**8**:53-57

[11] Kumar R, Chhatwal S, Arora S, Sharma S, Singh J, Singh N, Bhandari V, Khurana A. Antihyperglycemic, antihyperlipidemic, anti-inflammatory and adenosine deaminase-lowering effects of garlic in patients with type 2 diabetes mellitus with obesity. Diabetes, Metabolic Syndrome and Obesity: Targets and Therapy. 2013;**6**:49-56. DOI: 10.2147/DMSO.S38888

[12] Ashraf R, Aamir K, Shaikh AR, Ahmed T. Effects of garlic on dyslipidemia in patients with type 2 diabetes mellitus. Journal of Ayub Medical College, Abbottabad. 2005;**17**:60-64

[13] Eidi A, Eidi M, Esmaeili E. Antidiabetic effect of garlic (*Allium sativum* L.) in normal and streptozotocin-induced diabetic rats. Phytomedicine. 2006;**13**:624-629. DOI: 10.1016/j.phymed.2005.09.010

[14] Madkor HR, Mansour SW, Ramadan G. Modulatory effects of garlic, ginger, turmeric and their mixture on hyperglycemia, dyslipidemia and oxidative stress in streptozotocin-nicotinamide diabetic rats. British Journal of Nutrition. 2011;**105**:1210-1217. DOI: 10.1017/S0007114510004927

[15] Gómez-Arbeláez D, Lahera V, Oubiña P, Valero-Muñoz M, De las Heras N, Rodríguez Y, Garcia RG, Camacho PA, Jaramillo PL. Aged garlic extract improves adiponectin levels in subjects with metabolic syndrome: A double-blind, placebo-controlled, randomized, crossover study. Mediators of Inflammation. 2013;**2013**:1-6. DOI: 10.1155/2013/285795

[16] Aktaş G, Şit M, Tekçe H. Yeni adipokinler: Leptin, adiponektin ve omentin. Abant Medical Journal. 2013;**2**:56-62. DOI: 10.5505/abantmedj.2013.97269

[17] Padiya R, Khatua TN, Bagul PK, Kuncha M, Banerjee SK. Garlic improves insulin sensitivity and associated metabolic syndromes in fructose fed rats. Nutrition & Metabolism. 2011;**8**:53. DOI: 10.1186/1743-7075-8-53

[18] Kim M, Kim H. Effect of garlic on high fat induced obesity. Acta Biologica Hungarica. 2011;**62**:244-254. DOI: 10.1556/ABiol.62.2011.3.4

[19] Lee SJ, Hwang CR, Kang JR, Shin JH, Kang MJ, Sung NJ. Anti-obesity effect of red garlic composites in rats fed a high fat-cholesterol diet. Journal of Life Sciences. 2012;**22**:671-680. DOI: 10.5352/JLS.2012.22.5.671

[20] El-Demerdash FM, Yousef MI, El-Naga NA. Biochemical study on the hypoglycemic effects of onion and garlic in alloxan-induced diabetic rats. Food and Chemical Toxicology. 2005;**43**:57-63. DOI: 10.1016/j.fct.2004.08.012

[21] Eyo JE, Ozougwu JC, Echi PC. Hypoglycemic effects of *Allium cepa, Allium sativum* and *Zingiber officinale* aqueous extracts on alloxan-induced diabetic Rattus norvegicus. Medical Journal of Islamic World Academy of Sciences. 2011;**19**:121-126. DOI: 10.4314/br.v6i2.28672

[22] Ogunmodede OS, Saalu LC, Ogunlade B, Akunna GG, Oyewopo AO. An evaluation of the hypoglycemic, antioxidant and hepatoprotective potentials of onion (*Allium cepa* L.) on alloxan-induced diabetic rabbits. International Journal of Pharmacology. 2012;**8**:21-29. DOI: 10.3923/ijp.2012.21.29

[23] Yoshinari O, Shiojima Y, Igarashi K. Anti-obesity effects of onion extract in Zucker diabetic fatty rats. Nutrients. 2012;**4**:1518-1526. DOI: 10.3390/nu4101518

[24] Matsunaga S, Azuma K, Watanabe M, Tsuka T, Imagawa T, Osaki T, Okamoto Y. Onion peel tea ameliorates obesity and affects blood parameters in a mouse model of high-fat-diet-induced obesity. Experimental and Therapeutic Medicine. 2014;**7**:379-382. DOI: 10.3892/etm.2013.1433

[25] Ebrahimi-Mamaghani M, Saghafi-Asl M, Pirouzpanah S, Asghari-Jafarabadi M. Effects of raw red onion consumption on metabolic features in overweight or obese women with polycystic ovary syndrome: A randomized controlled clinical trial. The Journal of Obstetrics and Gynecology Research. 2014;**40**:1067-1076. DOI: 10.1111/jog.12311

[26] Naeem F, Khan SH. Purslane (*Portulaca oleracea* L.) as phytogenic substance—A review. Journal of Herbs, Spices & Medicinal Plants. 2013;**19**:216-232. DOI: 10.1080/10496475.2013.782381

[27] Bolkent Ş, Yanardağ R, Tabakoğlu-Oğuz A, Özsoy-Saçan Ö. Effects of chard (*Beta vulgaris* L. var. cicla) extract on pancreatic B cells in streptozotocin-diabetic rats: A morphological and biochemical study. Journal of Ethnopharmacology. 2000;**73**:251-259. DOI: 10.1016/S0378-8741(00)00328-7

[28] Sultana A, Rahman K. *Portulaca oleracea* Linn. A global panacea with ethno-medicinal and pharmacological potential. International Journal of Pharmacy and Pharmaceutical Sciences. 2013;**5**:33-39

[29] Wainstein J, Landau Z, Dayan YB, Jakubowicz D, Grothe T, Perrinjaquet-Moccetti T, Boaz M. Purslane extract and glucose homeostasis in adults with type 2 diabetes: A double-blind, placebo-controlled clinical trial of efficacy and safety. Journal of Medicinal Food. 2016;**19**:133-140. DOI: 10.1089/jmf.2015.0090

[30] El-Sayed MIK. Effects of *Portulaca oleracea* L. seeds in treatment of type-2 diabetes mellitus patients as adjunctive and alternative therapy. Journal of Ethnopharmacology. 2011;**137**:643-651. DOI: 10.1016/j.jep.2011.06.020

[31] Heidarzadeh S, Farzanegi P, Azarbayjani MA, Daliri R. Purslane effect on GLP-1 and GLP-1 receptor in type 2 diabetes. Electronic Physician. 2013;**5**:582-587. DOI: 10.14661/2013.582-587

[32] El-Newary SA. The hypolipidemic effect of *Portulaca oleracea* L. stem on hyperlipidemic Wister albino rats. Annals of Agricultural Sciences. 2016;**61**:111-124. DOI: 10.1016/j.aoas.2016.01.002

[33] Zidan Y, Bouderbala S, Djellouli F, Lacaille-Dubois MA, Bouchenak M. *Portulaca oleracea* reduces triglyceridemia, cholesterolemia, and improves lecithin: Cholesterol acyltransferase activity in rats fed enriched-cholesterol diet. Phytomedicine. 2014;**21**:1504-1508. DOI: 10.1016/j.phymed.2014.07.010

[34] Gu JF, Zheng ZY, Yuan JR, Zhao BJ, Wang CF, Zhang L, Xu QY, Yin QW, Feng L, Jia XB. Comparison on hypoglycemic and antioxidant activities of the fresh and dried *Portulaca oleracea* L. in insulin-resistant HepG2 cells and streptozotocin-induced C57BL/6J diabetic mice. Journal of Ethnopharmacology. 2015;**161**:214-223. DOI: 10.1016/j.jep.2014.12.002

[35] Samarghandian S, Borji A, Farkhondeh T. Attenuation of oxidative stress and inflammation by *Portulaca oleracea* in streptozotocin-induced diabetic rats. Journal of Evidence-Based Complementary & Alternative Medicine. 2017;**22**:562-566. DOI: 10.1177/2156587217692491

[36] Gezginci-Oktayoglu S, Sacan O, Bolkent S, Ipci Y, Kabasakal L, Sener G, Yanardag R. Chard (*Beta vulgaris* L. var. cicla) extract ameliorates hyperglycemia by increasing GLUT2 through Akt2 and antioxidant defense in the liver of rats. Acta Histochemica. 2014;**116**:32-39. DOI: 10.1016/j.acthis.2013.04.016

[37] Kabir AU, Samad MB, Ahmed A, Jahan MR, Akhter F, Tasnim J, Hannan JMA. Aqueous fraction of Beta vulgaris ameliorates hyperglycemia in diabetic mice due to enhanced glucose stimulated insulin secretion, mediated by acetylcholine and GLP-1, and elevated glucose uptake via increased membrane bound GLUT4 transporters. PLoS One. 2015;**10**:e0116546. DOI: 10.1371/journal.pone.0116546

[38] Hashem AN, Soliman MS, Hamed MA, Swilam NF, Lindequist U, Nawwar MA. Beta vulgaris subspecies cicla var. flavescens (Swiss chard): Flavonoids, hepatoprotective and hypolipidemic activities. Die Pharmazie - An International Journal of Pharmaceutical Sciences. 2016;**71**:227-232. DOI: 10.1691/ph.2016.5821

[39] Chang HP, Wang ML, Chan MH, Chiu YS, Chen YH. Antiobesity activities of indole-3-carbinol in high-fat-diet-induced obese mice. Nutrition. 2011;**27**:463-470. DOI: 10.1016/j.nut.2010.09.006

[40] Jayakumar P, Pugalendi KV, Sankaran M. Attenuation of hyperglycemia-mediated oxidative stress by indole-3-carbinol and its metabolite 3,3′-diindolylmethane in C57BL/6J mice. Journal of Physiology and Biochemistry. 2014;**70**:525-534. DOI: 10.1007/s13105-014-0332-5

[41] Lee JJ, Shin HD, Lee YM, Kim AR, Lee MY. Effect of broccoli sprouts on cholesterol-lowering and anti-obesity effects in rats fed high fat diet. Journal of the Korean Society of Food Science and Nutrition. 2009;**38**:309-318. DOI: 10.3746/jkfn.2009.38.3.309

[42] Mohamed S. Functional foods against metabolic syndrome (obesity, diabetes, hypertension and dyslipidemia) and cardiovasular disease. Trends in Food Science & Technology. 2014;**35**:114-128. DOI: 10.1016/j.tifs.2013.11.001

[43] Helmstädter A. Beans and diabetes: *Phaseolus vulgaris* preparations as antihyperglycemic agents. Journal of Medicinal Food. 2010;**13**:251-254. DOI: 10.1089/jmf.2009.0002

[44] Rebello CJ, Greenway FL, Finley JW. A review of the nutritional value of legumes and their effects on obesity and its related co-morbidities. Obesity Reviews. 2014;**15**:392-407. DOI: 10.1111/obr.12144

[45] Lozano R, Naghavi M, Foreman K, Lim S, Shibuya K, Aboyans V, Abraham J, Adair T, Aggarwal R, Ahn SY, AlMazroa MA, Alvarado M, Anderson R, Anderson L. Global and regional mortality from 235 causes of death for 20 age groups in 1990 and 2010: A systematic analysis for the global burden of disease study 2010. The Lancet. 2012;**380**: 2095-2128. DOI: 10.1016/S0140-6736(12)61728-0

[46] Roth GA, Forouzanfar MH, Moran AE, Barber R, Nguyen G, Feigin VL, Murray CJ. Demographic and epidemiologic drivers of global cardiovascular mortality. New England Journal of Medicine. 2015;**372**:1333-1341. DOI: 10.1056/NEJMoa1406656

[47] Radhika G, Sudha V, Sathya RM, Ganesan A, Mohan V. Association of fruit and vegetable intake with cardiovascular risk factors in urban south Indians. British Journal of Nutrition. 2008;**99**:398-405. DOI: 10.1017/S0007114507803965

[48] Kris-Etherton PM, Hecker KD, Bonanome A, Coval SM, Binkoski AE, Hilpert KF, Etherton TD. Bioactive compounds in foods: Their role in the prevention of cardiovascular disease and cancer. The American Journal of Medicine. 2002;**113**:71-88. DOI: 10.1016/S0002-9343(01)00995-0

[49] Yeh YY, Liu L. Cholesterol-lowering effect of garlic extracts and organosulfur compounds: Human and animal studies. The Journal of Nutrition. 2001;**131**:989-993. DOI: 10.1093/jn/131.3.989S

[50] Chang HS, Yamato O, Yamasaki M, Maede Y. Modulatory influence of sodium 2-propenyl thiosulfate from garlic on cyclooxygenase activity in canine platelets: Possible mechanism for the anti-aggregatory effect. Prostaglandins, Leukotrienes and Essential Fatty Acids. 2005;**72**:351-355. DOI: 10.1016/j.plefa.2005.01.003

[51] Moriguchi T, Takasugi N, Itakura Y. The effects of aged garlic extract on lipid peroxidation and the deformability of erythrocytes. The Journal of Nutrition. 2001;**131**:1016-1019. DOI: 10.1093/jn/131.3.1016S

[52] Ried K, Frank OR, Stocks NP. Aged garlic extract reduces blood pressure in hypertensives: A dose–response trial. European Journal of Clinical Nutrition. 2013;**67**:64-70. DOI: 10.1038/ejcn.2012.178

[53] Knekt P, Jarvinen R, Reunanen A, Maatela J. Flavonoid intake and coronary mortality in Finland: A cohort study. BMJ. 1996;**312**:478-481. DOI: 10.1136/bmj.312.7029.478

[54] Briggs WH, Folts JD, Osman HE, Goldman IL. Administration of raw onion inhibits platelet-mediated thrombosis in dogs. The Journal of Nutrition. 2001;**131**:2619-2622. DOI: 10.1093/jn/131.10.2619

[55] Colina-Coca C, González-Peña D, De Ancos B, Sánchez-Moreno C. Dietary onion ameliorates antioxidant defence, inflammatory response, and cardiovascular risk biomarkers in hypercholesterolemic Wistar rats. Journal of Functional Foods. 2017;**36**:300-309. DOI: 10.1016/j.jff.2017.07.014

[56] Joshipura KJ, Hu FB, Manson JE, Stampfer MJ, Rimm EB, Speizer FE, Willett WC. The effect of fruit and vegetable intake on risk for coronary heart disease. Annals of Internal Medicine. 2001;**134**:1106-1114. DOI: 10.7326/0003-4819-134-12-200106190-00010

[57] Lidder S, Webb AJ. Vascular effects of dietary nitrate (as found in green leafy vegetables and beetroot) via the nitrate-nitrite-nitric oxide pathway. British Journal of Clinical Pharmacology. 2013;**75**:677-696. DOI: 10.1111/j.1365-2125.2012.04420.x

[58] Huang T, Yang B, Zheng J, Li G, Wahlqvist ML, Li D. Cardiovascular disease mortality and cancer incidence in vegetarians: A meta-analysis and systematic review. Annals of Nutrition and Metabolism. 2012;**60**:233-240. DOI: 10.1159/000337301

[59] Larsson SC, Virtamo J, Wolk A. Total and specific fruit and vegetable consumption and risk of stroke: A prospective study. Atherosclerosis. 2013;**227**:147-152. DOI: 10.1016/j.atherosclerosis.2012.12.022

[60] Rastogi T, Reddy KS, Vaz M, Spiegelman D, Prabhakaran D, Willett WC, Ascherio A. Diet and risk of ischemic heart disease in India. The American Journal of Clinical Nutrition. 2004;**79**:582-592. DOI: 10.1093/ajcn/79.4.582

[61] Lundberg JO, Feelisch M, Björne H, Jansson EÅ, Weitzberg E. Cardioprotective effects of vegetables: Is nitrate the answer? Nitric Oxide. 2006;**15**:359-362. DOI: 10.1016/j.niox.2006.01.013

[62] Manchali S, Murthy KNC, Patil BS. Crucial facts about health benefits of popular cruciferous vegetables. Journal of Functional Foods. 2012;**4**:94-106. DOI: 10.1016/j.jff.2011.08.004

[63] Jeffery EH, Araya M. Physiological effects of broccoli consumption. Phytochemistry Reviews. 2009;**8**:283-298. DOI: 10.1007/s11101-008-9106-4

[64] Piao CS, Gao S, Lee GH, Park BH, Chae SW, Chae HJ, Kim SH. Sulforaphane protects ischemic injury of hearts through antioxidant pathway and mitochondrial KATP channels. Pharmacological Research. 2010;**61**:342-348. DOI: 10.1016/j.phrs.2009.11.009

[65] Blekkenhorst LC, Bondonno CP, Lewis JR, Devine A, Zhu K, Lim WH, Hodgson JM. Cruciferous and allium vegetable intakes are inversely associated with 15-year atherosclerotic vascular disease deaths in older adult women. Journal of the American Heart Association. 2017;**6**:e006558. DOI: 10.1161/JAHA.117.006558

[66] Zhang X, Shu XO, Xiang YB, Yang G, Li H, Gao J, Zheng W. Cruciferous vegetable consumption is associated with a reduced risk of total and cardiovascular disease mortality. The American Journal of Clinical Nutrition. 2011;**94**:240-246. DOI: 10.3945/ajcn.110.009340

[67] Saluk J, Bijak M, Kołodziejczyk-Czepas J, Posmyk M, Janas K, Wachowicz B. Anthocyanins from red cabbage extract—Evidence of protective effects on blood platelets. Open Life Sciences. 2012;**7**:655-663. DOI: 10.2478/s11535-012-0057-9

[68] Murashima M, Watanabe S, Zhuo XG, Uehara M, Kurashige A. Phase 1 study of multiple biomarkers for metabolism and oxidative stress after one-week intake of broccoli sprouts. BioFactors. 2004;**22**:271-275. DOI: 10.1002/biof.5520220154

[69] Bazzano LA, He J, Ogden LG, Loria C, Vupputuri S, Myers L, Whelton PK. Legume consumption and risk of coronary heart disease in US men and women: NHANES I epidemiologic follow-up study. Archives of Internal Medicine. 2001;**161**:2573-2578. DOI: 10.1001/archinte.161.21.2573

[70] Lattimer JM, Haub MD. Effects of dietary fiber and its components on metabolic health. Nutrients. 2010;**2**:1266-1289. DOI: 10.3390/nu2121266

[71] Shi J, Arunasalam K, Yeung D, Kakuda Y, Mittal G, Jiang Y. Saponins from edible legumes: Chemistry, processing, and health benefits. Journal of Medicinal Food. 2004;**7**:67-78. DOI: 10.1089/109662004322984734

[72] Menotti A, Kromhout D, Blackburn H, Fidanza F, Buzina R, Nissinen A. Food intake patterns and 25-year mortality from coronary heart disease: Cross-cultural correlations in the seven countries study. European Journal of Epidemiology. 1999;**15**:507-515

[73] Nöthlings U, Schulze MB, Weikert C, Boeing H, Van der Schouw YT, Bamia C, Peeters PH. Intake of vegetables, legumes, and fruit, and risk for all-cause, cardiovascular, and cancer mortality in a European diabetic population. The Journal of Nutrition. 2008;**138**:775-781. DOI: 10.1093/jn/138.4.775

[74] Insel P, Turner RE, Ross D. Diet and health. In: Insel P, Turner RE, Ross D, editors. Nutrition. 3rd ed. Jones and Barlett Publishers. 2007. Judbury, Massashusetts. pp. 598-640

[75] Heim KC, Spinalla MJ. In: Bagchi D, Preuss H, Swaropp A, editors. Nutraceuticals and Functional Foods in Human Health and Disease Prevention. 1st ed. CRP Press, Taylor Francis Group; 2016. Las Vegas. Pp. 361-390

[76] WHO (World Health Organization) [Internet]. 2018. Available from: http://www.who.int/dietphysicalactivity/fruit/en/ [Accessed February 8, 2018]

[77] Soh Y, Shin M, Lee J, Jang J, Kim OH, Kang H, Surh Y. Oxidative DNA damage and glioma cell death induced by tetrahydropapaveroline. Mutation Research. 2003;**544**: 129-142. DOI: 10.1016/j.mrrev.2003.06.023

[78] AICR (American Institute for Cancer Research [Internet]. 2015. Available from: http://www.aicr.org/ [Accessed: March 3, 2018]

[79] WHO (World Health Organization) [Internet]. 2018. Available from: http://www.who.int/elena/titles/fruit_vegetables_ncds/en/ [Accessed February 10, 2018]

[80] Wang Y, Li F, Wang Z, Qiu TQ, Shen Y, Wang M. Fruit and vegetable consumption and risk of lung cancer: A dose-response meta-analysis of prospective cohort studies. Lung Cancer. 2015;**88**(2):124-130. DOI: 10.1016/j.lungcan.2015.02.015

[81] Tang L, Lee AH, Su D, Binns CW. Fruit and vegetable consumption associated with reduced risk of epithelial ovarian cancer in southern Chinese women. Gynecologic Oncology. 2014;**132**:241-247. DOI: 10.1016/j.ygyno.2013.10.020

[82] Shigiharaa M, Obara T, Nagai M, Sugawara Y, Watanabe T, Kakizaki M, Nishino Y, Kuriyama S, Tsuji I. Consumption of fruits, vegetables, and seaweeds (sea vegetables) and pancreatic cancer risk: The Ohsaki cohort study. Cancer Epidemiology. 2014;**38**(2): 129-136. DOI: 10.1016/j.canep.2014.01.001

[83] NOA (National Onion Association) [Internet]. 2018. Available from: www.onions-usa.org [Accessed: February 5, 2018]

[84] Wang Y, Tian W, Ma X. Inhibitory effects of onion (*Allium cepa* L.) extract on proliferation of cancer cells and adipocytes via inhibiting fatty acid synthase. Asian Pacific Journal of Cancer Prevention. 2012;**13**:5573-5579. DOI: 10.7314/APJCP.2012.13.11.5573

[85] Das S. Garlic-A natural source of cancer preventive compounds. Asian Pacific Journal of Cancer Prevention. 2002;**3**:305-311

[86] Nicastro HL, Ross SA, Milner JA. Garlic and onions: Their cancer prevention properties. Cancer Prevention Research. 2015;**8**:181-190. DOI: 10.1158/1940-6207.CAPR-14-0172

[87] Fleischauer AT, Poole C, Arab L. Garlic consumption and cancer prevention: Meta-analyses of colorectal and stomach cancers. The American Journal of Clinical Nutrition. 2000;**72**:1047-1052

[88] Steiawan VW, Yu GP, Lu QY, Lu ML, Yu SZ, Mu L, Zhang JG, Kurtz RC, Cai L, Hsieh CC, Zhang ZF. Allium vegetables and stomach cancer risk in China. Communication Research. 2005;**6**:387-395

[89] Carlos J, Dias S. Nutritional and health benefits of carrots and their seed extracts. Food and Nutrition Sciences. 2014;**5**:2147-2156. DOI: 10.4236/fns.2014.522227

[90] Xu X, Cheng Y, Li S, Zhu Y, Xu X, Zheng X, Mao Q, Xie L. Dietary carrot consumption and the risk of prostate cancer. European Journal of Nutrition. 2014:1-9. DOI: 10.1007/s00394-014-0667-2

[91] Garti H. Effects of carrot consumption on intestinal cancer risk [thesis]. United Kingdom: Newcastle University; 2006

[92] Pollock RL. Comparing consumption of green leafy vegetables to cruciferous vegetables in relations to incidence of 17 different cancers: A meta- analysis. The Global Journal of Medical Research. 2016;**16**:30-39

[93] Tao J, Li Y, Li S, Li HB. Plant foods for the prevention and management of colon cancer. Journal of Functional Foods. 2018;**42**:95-110. DOI: 10.1016/j.jff.2017.12.064

[94] Tewani R, Sharma JK, Rao SV. Spinach (Palak) natural laxative. International Journal of Applied Research and Technology. 2016;**1**:140-148. DOI: 10.4172/2157-7471.1000110

[95] AND (Academy of Nutrition and Dietetics) [Internet]. 2018. Available from: https://www.eatright.org/food [Accessed February 2, 2018]

[96] Ullah MF. Sulforaphane (SFN): An isothiocyanate in a cancer chemoprevention paradigm. Medicine. 2015;**2**:141-156. DOI: 10.3390/medicines2030141

[97] Palak, Soni K, Thakur A, Kohli K. Broccoli: An insight into formulation and patentability aspects. Drug design. 2016;**5**:1-12. DOI: 10.4172/2169-0138.1000139

[98] Jang J, Surh Y. Potentiation of cellular antioxidant capacity by Bcl-2: Applications for its antiapoptotic function. Biochemical Pharmacology. 2003;(**8**):1371-1379. DOI: 10.1016/S0006-2952(03)00487-8

[99] Hadley CW, Miller EC, Schwartz SJ, Clinton SK. Tomatoes, lycopene, and prostate cancer. Progress and Promise. 2002:869-880. DOI: 1535-3702/02/22710-0869$15.00

[100] Palozza P, Simone RE, Catalano A, Mele MC. Tomato lycopene and lung cancer prevention: From experimental to human studies. Cancer. 2011;**3**:2333-2357. DOI: 10.3390/cancers3022333

[101] Clark R, Lee SH. Anticancer properties of capsaicin against human cancer. Anticancer Research. 2016;**36**:837-844

[102] Prodanov M, Sierra I, Vidal-Valverde C. Influence of soaking and cooking on the thiamin, riboflavin and niacin contents of legumes. Food Chemistry. 2004;**84**(2):271-277

[103] Murador D, Braga AR, Da Cunha D, De Rosso V. Alterations in phenolic compound levels and antioxidant activity in response to cooking technique effects: A meta-analytic investigation. Critical Reviews in Food Science and Nutrition. 2018;**58**(2):169-177

[104] Dos Reis LCR, de Oliveira VR, Hagen MEK, Jablonski A, Flôres SH, de Oliveira Rios A. Effect of cooking on the concentration of bioactive compounds in broccoli (*Brassica oleracea* var. avenger) and cauliflower (*Brassica oleracea* var. Alphina F1) grown in an organic system. Food Chemistry. 2015;**172**:770-777

[105] Rodrigues AS, Rosa EAS. Effect of post-harvest treatments on the level of glucosinolates in broccoli. Journal of the Science of Food and Agriculture. 1999;**79**:1028-1032

[106] Rehman ZU, Islam M, Shah WH. Effect of microwave and conventional cooking on insoluble dietary fibre components of vegetables. Food Chemistry. 2003;**80**:237-240

[107] Wachtel-Galor S, Wong KW, Benzie IFF. The effect of cooking on *Brassica* vegetables. Food Chemistry. 2008;**110**(3):706-710

[108] Bernhardt S, Schlich E. Impact of different cooking methods on food quality: Retention of lipophilic vitamins in fresh and frozen vegetables. Journal of Food Engineering. 2006;**77**(2):327-333

[109] Fabbri ADT, Crosby GA. A review of the impact of preparation and cooking on the nutritional quality of vegetables and legumes. International Journal of Gastronomy and Food Science. 2016;**3**:2-11

[110] Dini I, Tenore GC, Dini A. Effect of industrial and domestic processing on antioxidant properties of pumpkin pulp. LWT - Food Science and Technology. 2013;**53**(1):382-385

[111] Gahler S, Otto K, Bohm V. Alterations of vitamin C, total phenolics, and antioxidant capacity as affected by processing tomatoes to different products. Journal of Agricultural and Food Chemistry. 2003;**51**(27):7962-7968

[112] Van den Berg H, Faulks R, Fernando Granado H, Hirschberg J, Olmedilla B, Sandmann G, Southon S, Stahl W. The potential for the improvement of carotenoid levels in foods and the likely systemic effects. Journal of the Science of Food and Agriculture. 2000;**80**:880-912

[113] Porrini M, Riso P, Testolin G. Absorption of lycopene from single or daily portions of raw and processed tomato. British Journal of Nutrition. 1998;**80**:353-361

[114] Stahl W, Sies H. Uptake of lycopene and its geometrical-isomers isgreater from heat-processed than from unprocessed tomato juice in humans. The Journal of Nutrition. 1992;**122**:2161-2166

[115] Charlton KE, Patrick P, Dowling L, Khulani K, Jensen E. Ascorbic acid losses in vegetablesassociated with cook-chill food preparation. South African Journal of Clinical Nutrition. 2004;**17**(2):56-63

[116] Scott J, Rebeille F, Fletcher J. Folic acid and folates: The feasibility for nutritional enhancement in plant foods. Journal of the Science of Food and Agriculture. 2000;**80**:795-824

[117] Gennaro L, Leonardi C, Esposito F, Salucci M, Maiani G, Quaglia G, Fogliano VB. Flavonoid and carbohydrate contents in tropea red onions: Effects of homelike peeling and storage. Journal of Agricultural and Food Chemistry. 2002;**50**(7):1904-1910

[118] Ewald C, Fjelkner-Modig S, Johansson K, Sjöholm I, Akesson B. Effect of processing on major flavonoids in processed onions, green beans, and peas. Food Chemistry. 1999;**64**:231-235

[119] Lombard K, Peffley E, Geoffriau E, Thompson L, Herring A. Quercetin in onion (*Allium cepa* L.) after heat-treatment simulating home preparation. Journal of Food Composition and Analysis. 2005;**18**(6):571-581

[120] Tudela JA, Cantos E, Espin JC, Tomás-Barberán FA, Gil MI. Induction of antioxidant flavonol biosynthesis in fresh-cut potatoes. Effect of domestic cooking. Journal of Agricultural and Food Chemistry. 2002;**50**:5925-5931

[121] Andlauer W, Stumpf C, Hubert M, Rings A, Fürst P. Influence of cooking process on phenolic marker compounds of vegetables. International Journal for Vitamin and Nutrition Research. 2003;**73**:152-159

[122] Blessington T, Nzaramba MN, Scheuring DC, Hale AL, Reddivari L, Miller JC. Cooking methods and storage treatments of potato: Effects on carotenoids, antioxidant activity and phenolics. American Journal of Potato Research. 2010;**87**:479-491

[123] Brown CR, Durst RW, Wrolstad R, De Jong W. Variability of phytonutrient content of potato in relation to growing location and cooking method. Potato Research. 2008;**51**: 259-270

[124] Mattila P, Hellström J. Phenolic acids in potatoes, vegetables, and some of their products. Journal of Food Composition and Analysis. 2007;**20**:152-160

[125] Wu X, Beecher GR, Holden JM, Haytowitz DB, Gebhardt SE, Prior RL. Lipophilic and hydrophilic antioxidant capacities of common foods in the United States. Journal of Agricultural and Food Chemistry. 2004;**52**:4026-4037

[126] Bembem K, Sadana B. Effect of different cooking methods on the antioxidant components of carrot. Bioscience Discovery. 2014;**5**(1):112-116

[127] Mazzco T, N'Dri D, Chiavaro E, Visconti A, Fogliano V, Pellegrini N. Effect of two cooking procedures on phytochemical compounds, total antioxidant capacity and colour of selected frozen vegetables. Food Chemistry. 2011;**128**:627-633

[128] Pellegrini N, Chiavaro E, Gardana C, Mazzeo T, Contino D, Gallo M, Riso P, Fogliano V, Porrini M. Effect of different cooking methods on color, phytochemical concentration, and antioxidant capacity of raw and frozen *Brassica* vegetables. Journal of Agricultural and Food Chemistry. 2010;**58**:4310-4321

[129] Chang SK, Nagendra Prasad K, Amin I. Carotenoids retention in leafy vegetables based on cooking methods. International Food Research Journal. 2013;**20**(1):457-465

[130] Alvi S, Khan KM, Munir AS, Shahid M. Effect of peeling and cooking on nutrients in vegetables. Pakistan Journal of Nutrition. 2003;**2**(3):189-191

[131] Dolinsky M, Agostinho C, Ribeiro D, De Souza Rocha G, Barroso SG, Ferreira D, Polinati R, Ciarelli G, Fialho E. Effect of different cooking methods on the polyphenol concentration and antioxidant capacity of selected vegetables. Journal of Culinary Science & Technology. 2016;**14**(1):1-12

[132] Chuah AM, Lee Y-C, Yamaguchi T, Takamura H, Yin L-J, Matoba T. Effect of cooking on the antioxidant properties of coloured peppers. Food Chemistry. 2008;**111**:20-28

[133] Ferracane R, Pellegrini N, Visconti A, Graziani G, Chiavaro E, Miglio C, Fogliano V. Effects of different cooking methods on antioxidant profile, antioxidant capacity, and physical characteristics of artichoke. Journal of Agricultural and Food Chemistry. 2008;**56**:8601-8608

[134] Shams El-Din MHA, Abdel-Kader MM, Makhlouf SK, OSS M. Effect of some cooking methods on natural antioxidants and their activities in some *Brassica* vegetables. World Applied Sciences Journal. 2013;**26**(6):697-703

[135] Yuan G-F, Sun B, Yuan J, Wang Q-M. Effects of different cooking methods on health-promoting compounds of broccoli. Journal of Zhejiang University Science B. 2009;**10**(8): 580-588

[136] Bongoni R, Verkerk R, Steenbekkers B, Dekker M, Stiege M. Evaluation of different cooking conditions on broccoli (*Brassica oleracea* var. italica) to improve the nutritional value and consumer acceptance. Plant Foods for Human Nutrition. 2014;**69**(3):228-234

[137] Mahn A, Reyes A. An overview of health-promoting compounds of broccoli (*Brassica oleracea* var. italica) and the effect of processing. Journal of Food Science and Technology. 2012;**18**(6):503-514

[138] Stea TH, Johansson M, Jägerstad M, Frølich W. Retention of folates in cooked, stored and reheated peas, broccoli and potatoes for use in modern large-scale services systems. Food Chemistry. 2007;**101**(3):1095-1107

Chapter 3

Health Benefits of Fruits and Vegetables: Review from Sub-Saharan Africa

Abstract

A fruit is defined as the edible part of a plant that consists of the seeds and surrounding tissues, while vegetables are plants cultivated for their edible parts. Fruits and vegetables are important sources of micronutrients and dietary fibres and are components of a healthy diet, which help in preventing major diseases. Due to the fact that fruits and vegetables have health promoting properties, they contribute to dietary guidance. This chapter defines the basic concepts related to health benefits of fruits and vegetables, reviews the previous literature on health benefits of fruits and vegetables and enumerates the health benefits of some common fruits and vegetables. It also examined the dietary recommendation of fruits and vegetables in less developed countries as well as present situation of fruits and vegetables consumption with particular reference to sub-Saharan Africa.

Keywords: health, consumption, dietary guidance, fruits, vegetables

1. Introduction

A fruit is the mature ovary of a plant or the succulent edible part of woody plants, while vegetables are the edible portions of a plant that can be eaten such as the leaves, stem, tubers, roots and bulbs, the sweet and fleshy product of a tree or other plant that contains seed and can be eaten as food [1]. Nutritionally, fruits and vegetables are energy-dense foods containing vitamins, minerals, fibre and other bioactive compounds [2–5].

According to Mintah et al. [6], a fruit is the edible and fleshy seed-associated structures of certain plants, which could be sweet (such as apples, oranges, grapes, strawberries, juniper berries and bananas) or non-sweet (such as lemon and olives) in their raw forms [7, 8].

Moreover, FAO [9] revealed that "increasing fruit and vegetable consumption is a major public health challenge at the moment". The statement was made due to the micronutrient deficiencies being experienced worldwide which lead to nutritional disorders such as weakened immune systems, birth defects, mental and physical retardation, among others. These nutritional deficiencies occur as a result of low consumption of fruits and vegetables and also probably because of low knowledge of the nutritional values of fruits and vegetables [10, 11]. Thus, the relevance of this chapter is on the health benefits of fruits and vegetables.

2. Basic concepts related to health benefits of fruits and vegetables

There are several implications of the colours of fruits and vegetables, as observed during the Pacific Regional Workshop on Promotion of Fruits and Vegetables for health in 2014. The purple/blue colour of fruits and vegetables signifies their antioxidant properties and their ability to reduce the risks of cancer, stroke and heart disease. Beetroot and eggplant are good examples. Red colour in fruits and vegetables reduces the risk of cancer and improves heart health (as observed in tomato, watermelon, radish and red grapes). Orange/yellow-coloured ones contain carotenoids that help in maintaining healthy eyes (e.g. carrot, lemon, pineapple). Phytochemicals having antiviral and antibacterial properties as well as potassium are found in brown/white fruits and vegetables such as banana, garlic, onion and ginger, among others. In addition, the green-coloured fruits and vegetables have phytochemicals having anticancer properties such as broccoli, green apples, spinach, green pepper, lettuce and cucumber [12].

2.1. Health benefits of fruits and vegetables

Benefits obtainable from consumption of fruits and vegetables are greater life span [13], improved mental health [14], better cardiovascular health [15], reduced risks of some cancers [16] and weight management [17], among others.

In a study conducted in the USA, lower risk of obesity was observed among healthy middle-aged women who consume fruits and vegetables [18].

Specifically, fruits contain sufficient potassium, which are needed to reduce the effect of bone loss and occurrence of kidney stones [19]. Fruits assist in proper functioning of the brain as it stimulates the memory recall [6] and supplies the human body with fibre needed for a healthy digestive system [19, 20]. Fruits are also rich in dietary nutrients such as potassium, antioxidants and folic acid [21–23]; consumption of fruits guarantees optimum health, gives instant energy to the body and provides vitamins and minerals that are beneficial to body functioning [24].

In addition, vegetables are important as they help improve overall health, protect the vital organs of the body, assist in weight control, and promote healthy skin and hair. They also give abundant antioxidants that help keep diseases away from the body and aid in digestion by preventing constipation, haemorrhoids and diarrhoea [25].

2.2. Health benefits of some common fruits in sub-Saharan Africa

Citrus: Some of the fruits in this category are lime, lemon, orange, tangerine, pomelo and grape. They contain flavonoids, which are thought to contain some anticancer properties [24]. Flavonoids are antioxidants that could neutralise free radicals, protect from heart diseases and improve blood flow through the coronary arteries [26]. Citrus fruits are high in vitamin C and contain folate as well as thiamin. Vitamin C protects the body from free radicals that could destroy the body and helps in wound healing and holding blood vessels, tendons, ligaments and bone together. Thiamin is an important component of metabolism, while folate is required for cell division [27].

Orange

Lime

Mango: Mangoes are low in calories, high in fibre and can help avoid constipation while the fibre assists in metabolism by aiding the absorption of vitamins. The peels contain enzymes, which aid breaking down of carbohydrates, fats and proteins to form easily absorbable by the body. Mangoes contain magnesium, an electrolyte mineral that helps in regulating blood pressure, and vitamin A, a protective role in eye health, and help to protect the DNA structure. In addition, it helps in reducing age-related cognitive decline as well as damage from dangerous radiations. Consumption of mangoes prevents some forms of cancer due to its component —mangiferin that helps in functioning of the immune system. It also prevents the body from some diseases such as anaemia, asthma and atherosclerosis. Mangoes are good for repairing brain tissues as they reduce the effect of anxiety, depression and insomnia. Furthermore, consumption of mangoes improves the joint and skin; it also strengthens the bone [28].

Mango

Pawpaw: Pawpaws have low calorie content, soluble dietary fibre and do not contain cholesterol. They are high in vitamin C, vitamin A and flavonoids. Vitamin A helps to maintain healthy skin and eyes; folic acid, thiamin (vitamin B1), riboflavin and pyridoxine are all useful in body metabolism. Pawpaw seeds are also used in the treatment of stomach ache and ringworm infections [29].

Pawpaw

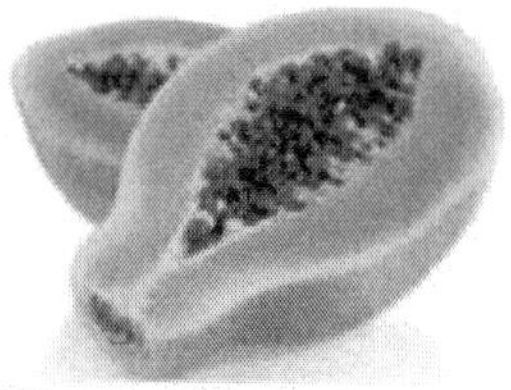

Sliced pawpaw

Pineapple: They contain calcium, potassium, carbohydrates, crude fibre and vitamin C (ascorbic acid, an effective antioxidant that aids the body's absorption of iron). It contains copper, which regulates the heart rate and blood pressure [30]. The vitamin C in pineapple also retards the development of urinary tract infections in pregnant women. Pineapples contain malic acid which boosts immunity and assists in maintaining oral health. They have natural anti-inflammatory properties and aids digestion. They are also a good source of manganese, a mineral that is required for building bones and connective tissues in the body [31]. Consumption of pineapple juice helps build healthy bones and restore the immune system. Moreover, consumption of pineapples helps the body to get rid of nausea, constipation, throat infections and intestinal worms.

Pineapple

Banana: It contains vitamins A, B6, C and D as well as potassium (that prevents muscle spasms). Banana helps the body to fight against ulcers; it is also useful in the treatment of anaemia, burns, wounds and arthritis. It aids constipation and presents a good relief for diarrhoea. Its main benefits include mood improvement, weight loss and promotion of the human muscles and bones [32].

Banana

Avocado: These fruits are creamy with high content of mono-unsaturated fats and are rich in dietary fibre and high in calories. They contain tannis which has anti-inflammatory and anti-ulcer properties. It also contains vitamins (A, E, K, folate, thiamin, niacin), minerals (iron, copper, magnesium, manganese) as well as potassium, which help regulate the heart rate and blood pressure [33].

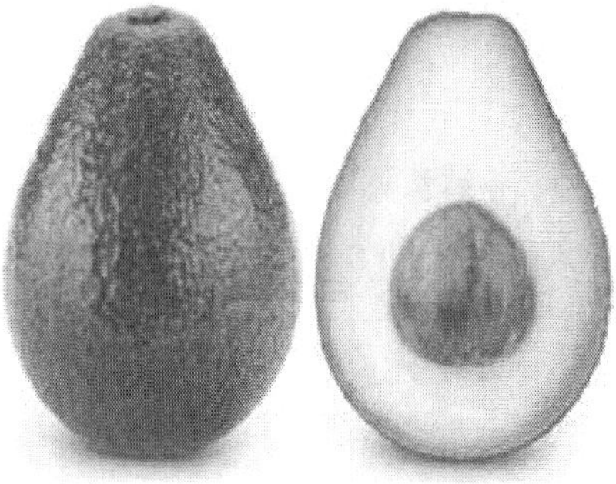

Avocado

African star apple: This fruit helps in lowering the blood sugar and cholesterol; a good treatment for toothache, constipation and sore throat. It is a good source of vitamin C which is a natural antioxidant and helps in weight loss. African star apple is low in carbohydrate, proteins, crude fibre and fat [34].

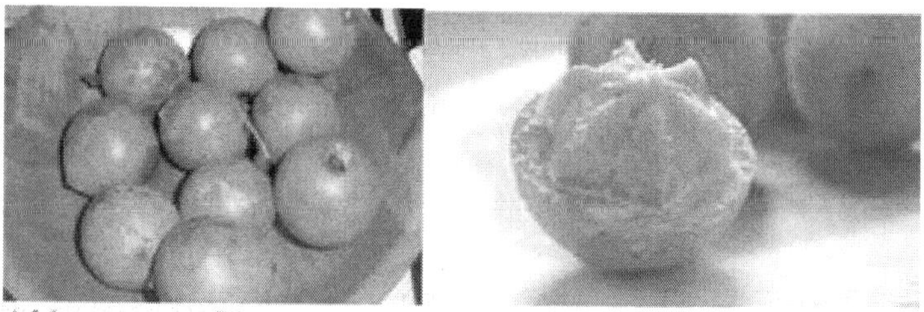

African star apple

Soursop: Soursop is used in the treatment of several ailments such as worms and parasites and as astringent for diarrhoea and dysentery. It is also used to cure cancer, improve the body's immune system, liver problems, kidney disease, urinary tract infections and prevents bacterial infections. Its consumption increases the milk production after childbirth in lactating mothers; its high vitamin C content is useful in slowing down the ageing process. It is rich in dietary fibre and contains calcium and magnesium needed for strong bones; contains vitamin B1 which aids in body metabolism and prevents nerve damage. It also has vitamin B2 which is needed for proper functioning of the nervous system and the body's energy production [35].

Soursop

Sweetsop/sugar apple: Consumption of this fruit facilitates milk production in lactating mothers, contains high amounts of folate required by pregnant women. It reduces the risk of heart attack and stroke as a result of the presence of high amount of magnesium. Vitamins A, B and C found in sweetsop makes it a good antioxidant and are needed for healthy skin. It regulates blood pressure level due to the presence of potassium in the fruits. Thiamin in sweetsop helps fight fatigue and weakness of the body. Its high content of calcium and magnesium assists in the promotion of healthy and strong bones; the niacin in sweetsop also controls body cholesterol level. The fruit also has anticancer properties, treats toothache and infections, prevents anaemia, promotes digestion and detoxifies the body [36].

Sweetsop/Sugar apple

African Bush mango: It is good for weight management, regulates cholesterol level and prevents constipation. This fruit is a rich source of potassium, iron, energy, protein, carbohydrates, ascorbic acid, sodium, dietary fibre, magnesium, calcium and phosphorus [37].

Africa bush mango seeds

Breadfruit: Consumption of breadfruits improves eye and bone health, immune system and physical cognitive condition [38]. It is high in carbohydrates, minerals, vitamins [39] and carotenoids [40]. Its consumption also protects the body against cancer, vitamin A deficiency, diabetes and heart disease. It is low in fat and cholesterol; a ready source of omega-3 and omega-6 fatty acids that regulate sebum production in the scalp and prevents hair loss. Consumption of breadfruit juice also improves the glowing of the skin, and the dietary fibre content of the fruit prevents heartburn, acidity, ulcer and gastritis as it eliminates toxic compounds from the gut [41].

Breadfruit

Guava: It is a super fruit rich in vitamins and minerals due to the bioactive compounds present in it. It has anti-allergenic, antimicrobial, anti-thrombotic and anti-artherogenic effects [42]. It also has antioxidants that help protect the body cells from damage.

Guava

Cashew: These nuts have high fat and calorie content and contain copper, which is useful for bone growth, nerve function and glucose metabolism. Most of the fat in cashew is in unsaturated form (oleic acid), which reduces triglycerides that could raise the risk of heart disease. Magnesium found in cashews is essential for energy generation, while zinc is important for reproduction and the immune system [43]. Consuming the nuts also prevents cancer and gall stones, strengthens the bones and promotes weight loss [44].

Cashew

Passion fruit: Its health benefits include promotion of intestinal health due to its high dietary fibre content; also it treats insomnia, helps during asthma attacks, kills cancer and reduces anxiety. It also aids weight loss and helps unwind the nerves. One serving of passion fruit provides the human body with the entire daily vitamin C requirement [45].

Passion fruit

Apples: Apples are rich in vitamins and minerals. Consuming these fruits aid weight loss, enhances brain health, provides antioxidants, reduces the risk of metabolic syndrome and prevents some forms of cancers [46].

Apples

Dates: Dates have high caloric content, low protein and fat content, moderate sources of vitamin A, adequate amounts of pyridoxine, niacin, pantothenic acid, riboflavin and vitamin K. They are also rich in minerals such as magnesium, manganese, selenium, potassium, copper, iron and calcium. The fruit cures anaemia, treats sexual weaknesses, night blindness, constipation and diarrhoea, prevents abdominal cancer and strengthens the human bones. It also helps maintain a healthy nervous system owing to the presence of potassium found in the cells and body fluids needed for the control of the body's heart rate and blood pressure level. Its iron content makes it suitable for pregnant women as it prevents haemorrhage after birth; it has anti-ageing benefits due to the presence of antioxidants that deals with harmful free radicals in the body [47].

Dates

2.3. Health benefits of some common vegetables in sub-Saharan Africa

Tomatoes: They contain the highest level of lycopene among all fruits and vegetables; lycopene is an antioxidant, which helps the body to get rid of free radicals that are harmful to it. Consumption of tomatoes helps in preventing various forms of cancers, reduces cholesterol level and thus reduces blood pressure due to the presence of vitamin B and potassium. Vitamin D in tomatoes keeps the hair shiny and strong, and it also helps improve vision. Chromium in tomatoes helps diabetic patients to keep the blood sugar level under control [48].

Tomatoes

Okra: Okra is a vegetable that contains vitamins (A, B1, B2, B3, B5, B6, B9 and C) and minerals (calcium, iron, phosphorus, potassium, magnesium, sodium and zinc). They also contain amino acids that are beneficial to health; lower cholesterol level; aid free bowel movement and reduce the risk of gastrointestinal problems. Consuming okra also contributes to active lifestyle. Okra contains antioxidants that remove free radicals from the body and potassium which helps reduce clotting and atherosclerosis. It has vitamin A that protects skin health, and high vitamin C content that induces the creation of white blood cells, which assists the immune system [49].

Okra

Eggplant: They have low carbohydrate and high fibre content, which helps the body manage blood sugar level. Its magnesium, calcium, phosphorus and potassium content helps to maintain the body's electrolyte balance. It helps to prevent birth defects in pregnant women due to its rich source of folic acid. It also contains iron and calcium that are both essential for bone health and aids in weight loss due to its low cholesterol content. Furthermore, it aids digestion because of its high dietary fibre content; iron and copper in eggplant also make it good in combating anaemia [50].

Eggplant

Cucumber: They contain sterols that can reduce cholesterol levels and as such, it is good in the treatment of both low and high blood pressure. Its consumption relieves arthritis pains and gout as well as promotes joint health. They are a good source of silica, which strengthens the connective tissues. Moreover, consuming cucumbers relieves bad breadth, helps in weight loss, aids digestion, fights some forms of cancer and helps rehydrate the body [51].

Cucumber

Pepper: They are appetite stimulants beneficial to people with starvation disorders. It also has antibacterial and anti-carcinogenic effects as well as good anti-inflammatory properties when applied topically [52].

Chili pepper

Watermelon: It has low calorie and a good source of vitamins and minerals. It provides lycopene, a powerful antioxidant along with vitamins A and C that have antioxidant and anti-ageing properties. It is an anti-inflammatory food that helps in limiting body stress, relieves pain, detoxifies the body and keeps skin healthy. It boosts immunity, manages high blood pressure, helps preventing kidney stones, boosts eye health, relieves acid reflux and helps fighting cancer [53].

Watermelon

Beets: Consumption of beets promotes cardiovascular well-being; it has high fibre content and improves exercise performance. The presence of antioxidants in beets is helpful in diabetic management, and it also boosts sex drive in men and women [54].

Beets

Garlic: Consumption of garlic helps reduce the risk of cancer and cardiovascular diseases, stimulates the immune function, restores physical strength and enhances detoxification [55].

Garlic

Onion: Onions protect the body from cardiovascular diseases, some infections and stomach cancer; it also improves lung function. It contains quercetin, which thins the blood, lowers cholesterol level, fights asthma, prevents blood clot, and acts as a sedative and an anti-inflammatory and anti-viral vegetable. Consumption of vegetables helps to detoxify the body, cures insomnia, improves the digestive system and memory and enhances strong nervous system [56].

Onion

Ginger: It is used to treat nausea and vomiting, lowers blood pressure, regulates blood glucose levels and also alleviates rheumatoid arthritis. It has antioxidant, antimicrobial and anticancer properties [57].

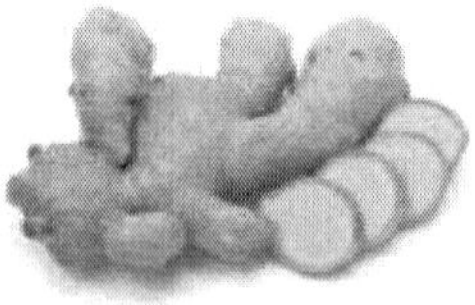

Ginger

2.4. Dietary recommendations of fruits and vegetables

Vegetables in particular are divided into food groups; the recommended daily intake is based on these groupings. The United States Department of Agriculture made it known that for these food groups, recommended daily intake should depend on the age, gender and level of activity of an individual. Vegetables have five subgroups which are as follows:

- Dark green vegetables, for example, broccoli
- Dark leafy green vegetables, for example, spinach
- Starchy vegetables, for example, green peas
- Beans and peas, for example, lentils
- Red and orange vegetables, for example, tomato, red pepper, carrot
- Other vegetables, for example, cabbage, beets, avocado, mushrooms

On the other hand, fruits are not divided into specific subgroups, but they also have recommended daily intake.

Recommended daily intake of vegetables for women of aged 50 and below is two and a half cup of vegetables, while men of the same age group require three cups of same vegetables. Once above 50 years, both men and women should reduce their daily intake by half a cup.

Recommended daily intake for fruits includes two cups of fruits for women up to 30 years of age and men of all ages, while beyond 30 years, women should reduce their daily intake to one and a half cup [58].

In less developed countries, minimum intake of 400 g of fruits and vegetables is required per day to prevent diseases and alleviate micronutrient deficiencies [2].

A study by [59] noted that recommended dietary guidelines should consider the consumer's age, sex as well as their physical activity level. The study showed a slight reduction in the percentage of adults in the United States who eat fruits and vegetables as opposed to the previous situation. According to the study, increased awareness on the benefits of fruits and vegetables consumption and educating people to change their eating behaviour are measures that could be put in place to ensure that people follow the recommended dietary guidelines. Other approaches could be employed such as farm-to-school programme, school gardening project and community projects.

2.5. Fruits and vegetables consumption in sub-Saharan Africa

There have been studies which examined fruits and vegetables consumption among different segments of the population in various parts of sub-Saharan Africa.

Fruits and vegetables consumption among younger population (adolescents in school) was examined by [60] in Cotonou, the Republic of Benin. It had earlier been observed in the area that most urban adults aged 35–64 years consume less than the recommended daily intake, while among school going adolescents, a mean daily intake of 97 g was observed for fruits and vegetables. This prompted a focus group discussion on the factors that determine fruits and vegetables in selected public and private schools in Cotonou. The choice of schools considered the parental income, class of the school children; as such, the schools were sampled from the most-disadvantaged and better-off neighbourhoods. From the discussion with the school students, they had not received information on consumption of fruits and vegetables (nutrition education) in school. They felt that unhealthy foods (sweets and biscuits) were as nutritious as fruits and vegetables. Two-thirds of students in the private schools opined that their parents purchased fruits and vegetables for them at home; on the other hand, only few of those in public schools attested to this. Moreover, parental influence was a major determinant of adolescent students' consumption of fruits and vegetables. Personal factors that influenced their consumption were preferences, their nutritional and health knowledge of the fruits and vegetables as well as cultural beliefs. Most of the students did not consume fruits and vegetables on a daily basis except for tomato and onions, which are mostly used in daily meals. Other factors such as food safety, cost of fruits and vegetables, medical prescription and media influence determine the adolescent students' consumption. The study concluded that to increase fruits and vegetables consumption among adolescents while in school, food vendors selling these products should be in and around the school. Also, parents play a major role, while adolescents from poor families should be targeted.

Another study by [61] also assessed the knowledge and consumption of fruits and vegetables among secondary school students in Lagos state, Nigeria. Most of the students have a good knowledge of the nutritional and health benefits of fruits and vegetables. However, only 5.45% of the students consumed the recommended daily intake of 400 g or five servings per day. As observed by the students, factors that could ensure adequate consumption of fruits and vegetables are parental intake, encouragement and supervision, availability and accessibility of fruits and vegetables at home. Therefore, the study opined that the school children should be encouraged to maintain healthy eating habits as they grow older.

In South Africa, Peltzer and Phaswana-Mafuya [62] conducted a study on fruits and vegetables consumption among older adults aged 50 years and above. It was a nationally conducted survey involving 3840 participants. The results of the survey showed that 68.5% of the older adults experienced insufficient fruits and vegetables intake as observed in their mean daily intake of four servings per day. Predictors of insufficient fruits and vegetables consumption included being a male, having low educational level, being overweight, lack of religious involvement, lower quality of life, daily tobacco use and being a black African/coloured participant. The study thus recommended public education and campaigns for increased fruits and vegetables consumption among older adults in South Africa.

In Ghana, Kpodo et al. [63] examined the consumption pattern and preferences of polytechnic students for fruits and vegetables. The study was conducted among 449 students with most of them (59.6%) consuming vegetables at least thrice a day, while only one-third of them consumed fruits 1–3 times daily. The most frequently consumed fruits among the polytechnic students were banana, mango and watermelon; while the least consumed were apples and pawpaw. For vegetables, tomato and onion were most frequently consumed; availability, convenience and cost were the three factors that mostly influenced the choice of vegetables consumed. Most of them purchase fruits (38.6%) and vegetables (45.8%) just sufficient for one serving, and they consumed these fruits and vegetables mostly for their known health benefits. Most preferred fruits included bananas, apples and watermelons, while vegetables such as carrots, tomatoes and onions were mostly preferred by the students for consumption. In essence, the study recommended that the fruits and vegetables mostly preferred by the students should be made available and accessible to them so as to change their eating habits. This is to ensure that they improve their consumption of fruits and vegetables.

Furthermore, a study by Layade and Adeoye [64] carried out an assessment of fruits and vegetables consumption among students of tertiary institutions in Oyo state, Nigeria. The study showed that the most preferred fruits by the students were banana and watermelon, while the least preferred were pawpaw and cashew. For vegetables, pumpkin leaves were the most preferred, while *Celosia argentea* was the least preferred vegetable. Health benefits, taste and availability were the major reasons for the students' preferences. Few of the students consumed the recommended daily intake of fruits and vegetables. Factors that affected the consumption of fruits and vegetables among the respondents were students' allowance, sex, parents allowance, availability and access. The study, therefore, recommended awareness creation to promote adequate consumption of fruits and vegetables among the study population.

Fruit intake level and its adequacy as well as determinants were examined by Ilesanmi et al. [65] among in-school adolescents in Nigeria. Fruit consumption among the female adolescents is lower than recommended. Adolescents with parents having high socioeconomic status had adequate fruit intake. The students' most preferred fruit was apple; while the study also showed that level of awareness of the benefits of fruits consumption for ensuring good health should be increased. Fruits should also be made available and affordable among adolescents to increase their consumption.

Also, a study was conducted by Mintah et al. [6], which examined the factors hindering fruits consumption among students in a public university in Ghana. Findings showed that high price and satiety were the most hindering factors for fruits and vegetables consumption. The low fruit intake was adjured to the fact that the consumption of fruits did not yield satisfaction for the students, that is, they could not eat fruits to alleviate hunger. Sixty five percent of the students did not consume up to the recommended daily intake of fruits and vegetables of 2–4 servings per day according to USDA 1992. Fruits such as oranges, apples, pineapple, pawpaw, banana, mango, pear, tangerine and watermelon were available to the students. The most preferred fruits were in descending order: pear, tangerine, apple, banana, guava, watermelon and pineapple. This study prescribed awareness creation and education on fruits consumption to improve public health, specifically among the university students and the general public as well.

In addition, Banwat et al. [66] assessed the consumption of fruits and vegetables among adults in an urban-slum in Jos Nigeria. Most of the respondents have fair knowledge of nutritional values; their knowledge of the nutritional values of fruits and vegetables was significantly determined by their sex and educational status. Most of them (69.2%) consumed adequate quantity of fruits and vegetables. Respondents gave the cost of food items and seasonal availability of fruits and vegetables as reasons for the low consumption. Thus, to improve the intake of fruits and vegetables in the study area, the mass media and health talks by health workers could be used to educate respondents on the need for them to increase their consumption. Moreover, to reduce the expenses on fruits and vegetables purchase, households were encouraged to have home gardens where they can produce the crops, which will ensure their availability and all year round consumption of fruits and vegetables.

The reviewed studies have shown the various factors affecting consumption of fruits and vegetables across different subpopulations within sub-Saharan Africa. Studies that were conducted among students (adolescents and tertiary institution students) revealed that consumption of fruits and vegetables was due to the knowledge of health benefits derived from them [60, 61, 63, 64]. Moreover, the reviewed studies recommended awareness creation [6, 64], public education campaign [62] and encouraging households to have home gardens where they can have access to fresh fruits and vegetables at reduced costs [66]. Most of the studies revealed that consumption of fruits and vegetables in the region is still below the recommended daily intake of five servings per day.

3. Conclusion

This chapter discussed the definition of fruits and vegetables, the concept of colour in fruits and vegetables and recommended daily intake of fruits and vegetables across the globe (which is the same world over). It also outlined the benefits of some common fruits and vegetables in the sub-Saharan region. In the same vein, the situation of fruits and vegetables consumption within the region was reviewed. The chapter thus concludes that, there is still more to be done in order for households in the region to meet the recommended daily intake of fruits and vegetables. As studies have highlighted, awareness creation and public campaigns in the form of health talks concerning the health benefits of consuming fruits and vegetables are important for the entire population to realise their benefits. In addition, a review of the health benefits of these fruits and vegetables shows that increasing their consumption will keep the entire household healthy. This is because consuming fruits and vegetables has been seen to prevent and cure several diseases which could be noticed among all the different population strata. This could be highlighted during awareness campaigns and health talks so as to encourage the public to consume more fruits and vegetables.

Conflict of interest

There is no conflict of interest on this document.

References

[1] UC Vegetable Research Information Center Frequently Asked Questions. Available from http://vric.ucdavis.edu/main/faqs.htm [Accessed: 2017-11-10]

[2] Agudo A. Measuring intake of fruits and vegetables. Background paper for the joint FAO/WHO Workshop on Fruit and Vegetables for Health; 1-3 September, 2004; Kobe, Japan

[3] World Cancer Research Fund. American Institute for Cancer Research. Expert report, food, nutrition, physical activity and the prevention of cancer: A global perspective. Available from http://www.dietandcancerreport.org/ [Accessed: 2007-11-26]

[4] Liu S, Manson JE, Lee IM, Cole SR, Hennekens CH, Willett WC, et al. Fruit and vegetable intake and risk of cardiovascular disease: The Women's health study. American Journal of Clinical Nutrition. 2000;**72**(4):922-928

[5] Van Duyn MA, Pivonka E. Overview of the health benefits of fruit and vegetable consumption for the dietetics professional: selected literature. J Am Diet Assoc. 2000;**100**(12): 1511-1521

[6] Mintah BK, Eliason AE, Nsiah M, Baah EM, Hagan E, Ofosu DB. Consumption of fruits among students: A case of Public University in Ghana. African Journal of Food, Agriculture, Nutrition and Development. April 2012;**12**(2):5979-5993. ISSN: 1684 5374

[7] Mauseth JD. Botany: An Introduction to Plant Biology. Massachusetts: Jones and Bartlett; 2003, 2003. pp. 271-272

[8] Lewis R. A CRC Dictionary of Agricultural Science. Florida: CRC Press; 2002. pp. 172-198

[9] FAO. Increasing fruit and vegetable consumption becomes a global priority. FAO News Room Focus 2003. 2003. Available from http://www.fao.org/english/newsroom/focus/2003/fruitveg1.htm [Accessed: 2017-11-28]

[10] Ruel MT, Nicholas M, Lisa S. Patterns and determinants of fruit and vegetable consumption in Sub-Saharan Africa. FAO/WHO workshop on fruits and vegetables for health, 1–3 September 2004. Japan. Available from www.who.mt../en/ [Accessed: 2011-5-21]

[11] Hart AD, Azubuike CU, Barimala SC. Vegetable consumption patterns of households in selected areas of the old rivers state of Nigeria. African Journal of Food Agriculture, Nutrition and Development. 2005;**5**(1). Available from http://www.ajfand.net/Volume5/No1/index1.html) [Accessed 2011-05-23]

[12] Hoejskov PS. Importance of fruit and vegetables for public health and food safety. Presentation at the Pacific Regional Workshop on Fruit and Vegetables for Health; PROFAV, Naji, Fiji; 20–23 October, 2014

[13] Bellavia A, Larsson SC, Bottai M, Wolk A, Orsini N. Fruit and vegetable consumption and all-cause mortality: A dose-response analysis. The American Journal of Clinical Nutrition. 2013 Aug 1;**98**(2):454-459. DOI: 10.3945/ajcn.112.056119. PMID: 23803880

[14] Conner TS, Brookie KL, Carr AC, Mainvil LA, Vissers MCM. Let them eat fruit! The effect of fruit and vegetable consumption on psychological well-being in young adults: A randomized controlled trial. PLoS One. 2017;**12**(2):e0171206. DOI: 10.1371/journal.pone.0171206

[15] Oyebode O, Gordon-Dseagu V, Walker A, Mindell JS. Fruit and vegetable consumption and all-cause, cancer and CVD mortality: Analysis of Health Survey for England data. Journal of Epidemiology and Community Health. 2014 Mar 31:jech-2013

[16] Boffetta P, Couto E, Wichmann J, Ferrari P, Trichopoulos D, Bueno-de-Mesquita HB, et al. Fruit and vegetable intake and overall cancer risk in the European Prospective Investigation into Cancer and Nutrition (EPIC). Journal of the National Cancer Institute. 2010 Apr 21;**102**(8):529-537. DOI: 10.1093/jnci/djq072. PMID: 20371762

[17] Rolls BJ, Ello-Martin JA, Tohill BC. What can intervention studies tell us about the relationship between fruit and vegetable consumption and weight management? Nutrition Review. 2004;**62**(1):1-17

[18] He K, FB Hu, GA Colditz, JE Manson, WC Willett, S Liu. Changes in intake of fruits and vegetables in relation to risk of obesity and weight gain among middle-aged women. International Journal of Obesity. 2004;**28**:1569-1574. DOI: 10.1038/sj.ijo.0802795

[19] USDA. Why is it important to eat fruit? Available from http://www.mypyramid.gov/pyramid/fruits_why.html. [Accessed: 2009-10-10]

[20] Ridgewell J. Examining Food and Nutrition. London: Oxford University Press; 1998. p. 58

[21] Tribble DL. Antioxidant consumption and risk of coronary heart disease, emphasis on vitamin C, vitamin E and beta-carotene; a statement for health care professionals from the American Heart Association. Circulation. 1999;**99**:591-595

[22] Ness AR, Powles JW. Fruit and vegetable and cardiovascular disease: A review. International Journal of Epidemiology. 1997;**26**:1-12

[23] Law MR, Morris JK. By how much does fruit and vegetable consumption reduce the risk of ischemic heart disease? European Journal of Clinical Nutrition. 1998;**52**:549-553

[24] Organic Facts. 5 Incredible Benefits of Fruits. 2018. Available from https://www.organicfacts.net/health-benefits/fruit [Accessed: 2018-01-11]

[25] Organic Facts. Benefits of Vegetables. 2018. Available from https://www.organicfacts.net/health-benefits/vegetable [Accessed: 2018-01-11]

[26] Kozlowska A, Szostak-Wegierek D. Flavonoids—Food sources and health benefits. Roczniki Państwowego Zakładu Higieny. 2014;**65**(2):79-85

[27] Dairy Council of California. Health Benefits of Fruits. 2017. Available from https://www.healthyeating.org/Healthy-Eating/All-Star-Foods/Frutis [Accessed: 2017-11-27]

[28] www.nutrition-and-you.com Mango fruit nutrition facts. Available from https://www.-nutrition-and-you.com/mango-fruit.html [Accessed: 2017-12-05]

[29] www.nutrition-and-you.com Papaya fruit nutrition facts. Available from https://www.-nutrition-and-you.com/papaya-fruit.html [Accessed: 2017-12-05]

[30] Debnath P, Dey P, Chanda A, Bhakta T. A survey on pineapple and its medicinal value. Scholars Academic Journal of Pharmacy. 2012;**1**(1):24-29

[31] Hossain MF, Akhtar S, Anwar M. Nutritional value and medicinal benefits of pineapple. International Journal of Nutrition and Food Sciences. 2015;**4**(1):84-88. DOI: 10.11648/j.ijnfs.20150401.22

[32] Sampath Kumar KP, Debjit Bhowmik, Duraivel S, Umadevi M. Traditional and medicinal uses of banana. Journal of Pharmacognosy and Phytochemistry. 2012;**1**(3):51-63. ISSN 2278–4136. Online Available at www.phytojournal.com

[33] www.nutrition-and-you.com Avocados Nutrition Facts. Available from https://www.-nutrition-and-you.com/avocados.html [Accessed: 2017-12-01]

[34] www.DrHealthBenefits.com 10 Health Benefits of African Star Aple based on Research. Available from https://drhealthbenefits.com/food-bevarages/fruits/health-benefits-african-star-apple [Accessed: 2017-12-01]

[35] Trupti PS, Dongre RS. Bio-chemical compositional analysis of *Annona muricata*: A miracle fruit's review. International Journal of Universal Pharmacy and Bio Sciences. March–April 2014;**3**(2):82-104. International Standard Serial Number (ISSN): 2319–8141

[36] Global Food Books. 24-mind blowing reasons you need sugar apple (sweet sop). 2017. Availabe from https://globalfoodbook.com/benefits-of-sugar-apple-fruit [Accessed: 2017-12-01]

[37] Global Food Books. 20 Key benefits of Ogbono-*Irvingia gabonensis*. 2017. Available from: https://globalfoodbook.com/20-key-benefits-of-ogbono-irvingia-gabonensis [Accessed: 2017-12-02]

[38] Tucker K. Nutrition concerns for aging population. In: Pray L, Boon C, Miller EA, Pillsbury L, editors. Providing Healthy Safe Foods As We Age. Workshop Summary. pp. 87-108

[39] Engelberger L, Alfred J, Lorens A, Iuta T. Screening of selected breadfruit cultivars for carotenoids and related health benefits in Micronesia. Acta Horticulurae. 2007;**757**:193-200

[40] Beyer K. Breadfruit as a candidate for processing. Acta Horticulturae. **757**:209-214

[41] www.moa.gov. Health Benefits of Breadfruits. 2017. Available from: www.moa.gov.jm/EatWhatWeGrow/data/BreadfruitHealthBenefitsfinal.pdf [Accessed: 2017-12-02]

[42] Mitra SK. Guava as a super fruit. Presentation of the chairman for the section of tropical and subtropical fruits; International Society for Horticultural Science. 2015. Available from: www.itfnet.org/download/tfnetsymposium2015/5-India.pdf [Accessed: 2017-12-02]

[43] www.nutsite.com Cashew Nutrition Facts. Available from www.nutsite.com/pdf/cashew_fact_sheet.pdf [Accesssed: 2017-12-02]

[44] www.tropicalfruits.com. Cashew Nut. Available from www.trpicalfruits.com/my/pdf/cashew-Nut-k-fruit.pdf [Accessed: 2017-12-02]

[45] Kumari S, Mishra PK. Passion fruit (*Passiflora edulis* Sims.)—An underexploited plant of nutraceutical value. Asian Journal of Medical and Health Research. 2016;**1**(4):1-10

[46] www.USApple.org Apple Health Benefits. U.S Apple Association. July 2010. Available from www.usapple.org [Accesssed: 2017-12-02]

[47] www.healthbeckon.com 18 Benfits of Date Fruit and Its Nutritional Value. 2014. Available from https://www.healthbeckon.com/date-fruit-benefits/vegetables [Accsssed: 2017-12-02]

[48] Bhowmik D, Sampath Kumar KP, Paswan S, Srivastava S. Tomato—A natural medicine and its health benefits. Journal of Pharmacognosy and Phytochemistry. 2012;**1**(1):33-43

[49] Healthbenefitstimes. Okra—*Abelmoschus esculentus*. 2017. Available from https://www.healthbenefitstimes.com [Accessed: 2017-12-03]

[50] Healthbenefitstimes. Eggplant—*Solanum melongena*. 2017. Available from https://www.healthbenefitstimes.com/eggplant/ [Accessed: 2017-12-03]

[51] Hang the bankers. 10 health benefits of cucumbers. 2012. Available from http://www.hangthebankers.com/10-health-benefits-of-cucumbers/ [Accessed: 2017-12-03]

[52] Reynolds C. Are Chile peppers good for your health? Retrieved from https://www.fatalii.net/Chiles-and-health on 4th December 2017

[53] Conscious Life News. 10 surprising health benefits of watermelon. 2017. Available from https://consciouslifenews.com/10-surprising-health-benefits-watermelon/1187059/ [Accessed: 2017-12-03]

[54] Simoloka and Bhikha. Beets health benefits. 2016. Available from https://tibb.co.za/articles/beets-health-benefits.pdf [Accessed: 2017-12-03]

[55] Roy H, Lundy S, Kalicki B. Health Benefits of Garlic. Pennigton Nutrition Series. Baton Rouge, Louisiana, USA: Pennington Biomedical Research Center; 2009. 4 pp

[56] Sharma A. Nutritional Benefits of Onion. India: Facts For You; April 2014. pp. 27-30. www.ffymag.com

[57] Singletary K. Ginger: An overview of health benefits. Nutrition Today. 2010;**45**(4):171-183

[58] SFGATE. Recommended Fruit and Vegetable Intake. Available from http://healthyeating.sfgate.com/recommended-fruit-vegetable-intake-4115.html [Accessed: 2017-12-05]

[59] Blanck HM, Gillespie C, Kimmons JE, Seymour JD, Serdula MK. Trends in fruit and vegetable consumption among U.S. men and women, 1994–2005. Preventive Chronic Diseases. 2008;**5**(2):1-10

[60] Nago ES, Verstraeten R, Lachat CK, Dossa RA, Kolsteren PW. Food safety is a key determinant of fruit and vegetable consumption in urban Beninese adolescents. Journal of Nutrition Education and Behaviour. 2012;**44**(6):548-555. DOI: 10.1016.j.jneb.2011.06.006

[61] Silva OO, Ayankogbe OO, Odugbemi TO. Knowledge and consumption of fruits and vegetables among secondary school students of Obele Community Junior High School, Surulere, Lagos State, Nigeria. Journal of Clinical Sciences. 2017;**14**:68-73. [Downloaded free from http://www.jcsjournal.org on Tuesday, November 28, 2017, IP: 197.211.57.115]

[62] Peltzer K, Phaswana-Mafuya N. Fruit and vegetable intake and associated factors in older adults in South Africa. Global Health Action. 2012;**5**:18668. DOI: 10.3402/gha.v5i0.18668

[63] Kpodo FM, Mensah C, Dzah CS. Fruit and vegetable consumption patterns and preferences of students in a Ghanaian polytechnic. World Journal of Nutrition and Health. 2015; **3**(3):53-59. DOI: 10.12691/jnh-3-3-2

[64] Layade AA, Adeoye IB. Fruit and vegetable consumption among students of tertiary institutions in Oyo state. Russian Journal of Agricultural and Socio-Economic Sciences. June 2014;**30**(6):3-8

[65] Ilesanmi OS, Ilesanmi FF, Ijarotimi IT. Determinants of fruit consumption among In-school adolescents in Ibadan, south West Nigeria. European Journal of Nutrition & Food Safety. 2014;**4**(2):100-109

[66] Banwat ME, Albert Lar L, Daboer J, Audu S, Lassa S. Knowledge and intake of fruit and vegetables consumption among adults in an urban community in north central Nigeria. The Nigerian Health Journal. January–March 2012;**12**(1):12-15

Chapter 4

Hydroponic Production Systems: Impact on Nutritional Status and Bioactive Compounds of Fresh Vegetables

Abstract

Hydroponic systems for vegetable production are nowadays essential to maximize productions and increase yields. Although the technical issues concerning the production are well explored and discussed, less information is available about the impact of hydroponic methods in the nutritional status of fresh vegetables and in particularly in their levels of bioactive compounds. Therefore, the aim of the current chapter is to provide accurate and updated information about their effects on compositional and bioactive properties of vegetables, comparing with conventional production mode. This chapter will be divided as the following sections: (1) introduction (introduction to the theme), (2) hydroponics and quality of vegetable produces, and (3) conclusion. With this chapter, we hope to present an updated and credible discussion, compare hydroponic versus conventional vegetables production mode, and present new consumers and producer trends.

Keywords: hydroponics, conventional production, nutrients, bioactivities

1. Introduction

Hydroponics can be briefly defined as cultivation of plants without soil [13]. In short, hydroponics, a Greek word meaning "hydro" (water) and "ponos" (labor) is the method of growing plants in different types of substrates (chemically inert), sand, gravel, or liquid (water), in which nutrients are added, but no soil is used [13, 14].

Actually, Europe is considered the biggest market for hydroponics in which France, the Netherlands, and Spain are the three top producers, followed by the United States of America and Asia-Pacific region. These systems are becoming increasingly widespread over the world, and according to the most recent report [15], it is expected to reach a world growth of 18.8% from 2017 to 2023, corresponding to a global hydroponic market USD 490.50 Million by 2023.

According to growers, hydroponic systems help them in expanding their ability for a continuous production in a short growing period, require less space, and plants can be produced anywhere, i.e., in a small spaces with a controlled growth environment [16]. Growers often reply that hydroponics always allows them to have higher productivities and yields without any constrains of climate and weather conditions [17]. In addition, growers often claimed that quality of hydroponic produces is superior because it uses a highly controlled environment and enables a more homogeneous production without any loss of water and nutrients. Moreover, hydroponics is not dependent on seasonality, and therefore, their productivities are higher and homogenous throughout the year [18]. Growers also often report that hydroponic productions are easier, and since they do not require cultural operations such as plowing, weeding, soil fertilization, and crop rotation, they are light and clean [19]. However, the scientific evidences are often contradictory and different disadvantages are reported to justify their rejection: high initial costs, high technical and plant physiology knowledge, periodic work routines, and efficient electrical systems [4, 19, 20]. It is also necessary and effective to control nutritional solutions and take daily measurements of liquid nutrients to avoid excess salinization and control microbial diseases and pests to avoid any loss of production [4]. Nonetheless, growers often argue that this technique allows the possibility to grow healthier food and helps in the reduction of wastes. An example of this waste reduction can be seen in lettuce, the most hydroponically cultivated crop in the world, in which about 99% of their hydroponic leaves are valid and they can be sold to a value approximately of 40% more expensive than a lettuce grown traditionally [4]. Moreover, with hydroponics, there is a better opportunity to place the fresh produces in the market since their average nutritional quality and consumer's acceptance are higher [21]. In addition, growers reported that with hydroponics, some of the negative impacts of conventional agriculture are avoided including high and inefficient use of water, large land requirements, high concentrations of nutrients and pesticides, and soil degradation accompanied by erosion [22, 23]; issues that are much more in the nowadays concerns of consumers.

Worldwide consumers are increasingly interested in having more environment-friendly fresh vegetables due to the strong and well-established inverse relationship between vegetable consumption and the risk of many types of chronic and degenerative diseases like cancer, cardiovascular, and neurological disorders [1]. Because of this growing consumer interest, the content of health-promoting compounds is becoming a vital consideration for fruit and vegetable growers. In fact, fresh vegetables and fruits are rich sources of bioactive compounds with significant health benefits, and these beneficial compounds can be influenced by several key factors including genotype selection and environmental conditions (light, temperature, humidity, atmospheric CO_2). Contrary to the conventional agricultural system, hydroponic relies on the manipulation of nutrients, which according to different authors allows having produces with high accumulation of some beneficial nutrients [3, 5]. However, questions about their safety are often raised.

There are considerable research studies regarding conventional and hydroponic production separately, but few have compared the impact of both on the nutritional quality of fresh vegetables. In this context, with this chapter, we discuss with updated information on the differences between of hydroponics and conventional production and the impact of hydroponics in the nutritional composition and bioactive compound levels. We debate their impact, limitations, and success.

2. Hydroponics and quality of vegetable produces

2.1. Hydroponic systems: Definition of hydroponics and brief description of main hydroponic systems

Hydroponic production is the method of growing plants under soilless (i.e., soil less) conditions with nutrients, water, and an inert medium (gravel, sand, pearlite among others) [13, 14].

From the perspective of plant science, there are no differences between soilless and soil-grown plants, because in both systems, the nutrients must be dissolved in water before plants can absorb them [24]. The differences reside in the way of nutrients that are available to the plants. In hydroponics, the nutrients are dissolved in water and the solution goes into the plant roots, which uptake the water with minerals toward different parts of plant. In the soil-based production, the elements stick to the soil particles, pass into the soil solution, where they are absorbed by the plant roots [24, 25].

There are different types of hydroponics, depending on how they are characterized. One criterion is to classify as closed or open hydroponic systems [25, 26]. The hydroponic systems that do not use growing media are usually referred as closed systems, while hydroponic systems with growing media in a container may be closed or open depending on whether the nutrient solution is recirculated (closed) or is introduced on every irrigation cycle (open). In the closed systems, the nutrient concentrations are constantly recycled, monitored, and adjusted, while in open systems, the nutrient solution is discarded (but stored) after each nutrition cycle.

Another approach to classify hydroponic systems is to classify them based on the movement of the nutrient solution: active or passive [26, 27]. Active means that nutrient solution will be moved, usually by a pump, and passive relies on a wick or the anchor of the growing media. Others characterize the hydroponics with recovery or nonrecovery criteria [26, 27]. Recovery is when the nutrient solution will be reintroduced into the system, while nonrecovery means that nutrient solution is applied to the growing media and vanish after that.

Although there is a large diversity of criteria, there are three fundamental things for plants: (1) water/moisture, (2) nutrients, and (3) oxygen. All these different types of hydroponics must deliver those three important fundamental things to achieve success in plant production. Despite this diversity, the criteria most commonly used by growers, farmers, private companies, and researchers categorize hydroponic systems into six different types [26–28]: Nutrient film technique (NFT), wick system, ebb and flow (flood and drain), water culture, drip system, and aeroponic system. **Table 1** summarizes the main characteristics of each system.

2.2. Bioactive compounds

2.2.1. *Definition of "bioactive compounds"*

According to Biesalski et al. [2], it is widely accepted that bioactive compounds can be defined as essential and nonessential compounds that occur in nature as part of the food chain and with positive effect on human health. Bioactive compounds consist of chemicals found in small volumes in plants (leaves, roots, shoots, bark) and foods such as fruits, vegetables, nuts, oils, cereals, and grains [29]. Bioactive compounds result from secondary metabolites of plants and are not essential for their daily functioning but play a significant role in the defense, attraction, signaling, and competition and thus are often named as secondary plant metabolites [30, 31].

2.2.2. *Types and main groups of bioactive compounds in vegetables*

Bioactive compounds may be classified according to different criteria. The most common classification used by literature is based on their pharmacological and toxicological effect. However, this is more relevant to the clinicians, pharmacist, or toxicologists and not for plant biologists, agronomists, or other researchers involved in plant-related studies. For these last groups, it is normal to classify them according to biochemical pathways and chemical classes.

Table 2 summarizes the main classes of bioactive compounds often found in plants and foods.

Hydroponic system	Description
Aeroponics	This is the most sophisticated and high-tech method, in which plants are suspended in special trails. Nutrients are sprayed, every few minutes, directly to the roots, which provide a light layer of nutrients. This system requires a regular monitorization of pumps to avoid any failure.
Deepwater culture (DWC)	In a DWC system, a reservoir is used to hold the nutrient solution. The roots of plants are suspended the nutrient solution in order to get a constant supply of water, oxygen, and nutrients. In this system, an air pump is used to oxygenate the water, preventing the roots from drowning.
Drip system	In this system, the nutrient solution is set apart in a reservoir, and the plants are grown separately in a soilless medium. Drip systems dispense nutrients at a very slow rate, through nozzles, and the extra solutions can be collected and recirculated, or even allowed to drain out. With this system, it is possible to simultaneously grow several kinds of plants.
Ebb and flow	Also known as "flood and drain," is the less-commonly used system in hydroponics. This system utilizes a grow tray and a reservoir that is filled with a nutrient solution. A pump periodically floods the grow tray with nutrient solution, which then slowly drains away. In this system, plants are normally grown in mediums like rockwool or gravel, but if they need a substantial amount of moisture, this is substituted with vermiculite or coconut fiber due to their high capacity of excess moisture retention between floodings.
Nutrient film technique (NFT)	Similar to aeroponics, the nutrient film technique (NFT) is the most popular hydroponic system. In this method, a nutrient solution is pumped constantly through channels in which plants are placed. When the nutrient solutions reach the end of the channel, they are sent back to the beginning of the system. This makes it a recirculating system, but unlike DWC, the plants roots are not completely submerged, which is the main reason for naming this method NFT.
Wick system	This is the easiest and simple method of hydroponics. It is a completely passive system, which means that nutrients are stored in a reservoir and moved into the root system by capillary action. With this system, we can find a diverse variety of growing medium such as perlite, vermiculite, coconut fiber, and other formulations. The wick system is easy and inexpensive to set-up and maintain. The biggest drawback of this system resides in the poor oxygenation of plant roots and the large amount of nutrient solution that is required to reach efficiently to the plant root system.

Table 1. Main types of hydroponic systems and their respective characteristics, according to growers, farmers, private companies, and researchers [18–20].

Chemical class	Health benefits	Example of primary food sources
Vitamins (C, E, and K)	Antioxidative protection of cells and membranes against reactive oxygen species (ROS), protection of lipoproteins, stabilization of cell membrane structures, modulation of immune response, inhibition of tumor growth in humans.	Fruits and vegetables.
Glycosides (cardiac glycosides, cyanogenic glycosides, glucosinolates, and anthraquinone glycosides)	Recent reports provide a large number of evidences about the chemopreventive role of different type of glycosides against cancers (bladder, prostate, esophagus, and stomach) and cancerous deleterious degenerative diseases. The glucosinolates, one of the most relevant group of glycoside compounds, are capable to activate enzymes involved in the detoxification of carcinogens, thus providing protection against oxidative damage.	Cruciferous vegetables, garlic, leek, onion.
Phenolics (natural monophenols and polyphenols including phenolic acids, flavonoids, aurones, chalconoids, flavonolignans, lignans, stilbenes, curcuminoids, and tannins)	The specific action of each phenolic is difficult to assess, because organisms absorb only a small part of it and in addition, they may suffer transformations. Epidemiological studies have claimed that polyphenols are capable of scavenging reactive oxygen species (ROS), inhibiting the peroxidation lipids from cellular membranes, preventing the LDL cholesterol from oxidation, and protecting DNA from mutations and oxidations.	Fruits and vegetables, tea, cocoa, wine, grapes, peanuts.
Carotenoids (carotenoids endowed with provitamin A activity, which are vital components of the human diet)	Although their bioactive mechanisms are still poorly understood, the heath importance of carotenoids is normally discussed in terms of antioxidant properties. Carotenoid-rich diets are correlated with a significant reduction in the risk of certain cancers, and heart and degenerative diseases. Epidemiological studies have shown that carotenoids may have anticancer and antimutagenic properties.	Green, orange, red, and yellow vegetables.
Plant sterols (phytosterols)	They regulate the fluidity and permeability of the phospholipid bilayers of plant membranes. Plant sterols have been hypothesized to have anticancer, antiatherosclerosis, anti-inflammation, and antioxidant activities.	Cruciferous vegetables, spinach, rice, soybean, wheat germ, wheat bran, nuts, and vegetable seeds.
Alkaloids (morphine, cocaine, solanine caffeine)	Morphine, cocaine, solanine, and caffeine are the most relevant alkaloids in plants. Besides the toxicity and their addictive effect, morphine and cocaine have been used in different formulations as anesthetics. The caffeine, the most known alkaloid and in high concentrations, is toxic and protects the plant seedlings from pests and plagues and prevents the germination of any other plants in the area (allopathic effects). In humans, caffeine has also been thought to reduce the risk of diabetes and heart disease, and recently, it has been associated with prevention of Alzheimer and Parkinson's diseases.	Papaveraceae (poppy family), coffee, cocoa, tea, Solanaceae (nightshade family), sweet peppers, chili peppers, jalapeno peppers eggplant, tomatoes, potatoes *Atropa belladonna* (deadly nightshade), *Datura* spp (thorn apples).
Saponins	Among other properties, saponins are referred as having cardioprotective and hepatoprotective effects. Saponins have been observed to reduce blood cholesterol, stimulate the immune system, and inhibit the growth of cancer cells.	Beans, grains, chickpeas, oats, quinoa, asparagus, soy, red wine, and melons.

Table 2. Main classes of bioactive compounds commonly found in plants, classified according to chemical class criteria [1, 2, 24–26].

2.3. Hydroponic and accumulation of bioactive compounds

Soil farmers experience these same types of variations with respect to soil health and fluctuations in environmental conditions. For example, water quality and variations in temperature and humidity can place stress on crops potentially changing their biochemical makeup regardless of the growing method being used. Because of these variations, studies to date comparing the nutritional content of produces grown hydroponically to soil grown have had mixed results, with some studies showing no difference between the two methods, while others showing that soilless systems fared either better or worse than soil-grown controls in the nutrient levels being tested. As you can imagine, experimental design and conditions vary widely between these studies and depend on how they were designed affecting the outcome and the significance of the findings.

Different studies have claimed that vegetables produced from hydroponics have better qualities than those from conventional soil-based cultivation [32, 33]. On the other hand, other studies have claimed that the exact differences between qualities of vegetables grown in soil or hydroponics are difficult to establish [10, 34, 35]. Nonetheless, all authors in general seem to agree that hydroponic systems can be the best alternative when arable soil is scarce or their types are not ideal for the desired crop.

Although there are diverse and contradictory opinions, the general view of researcher seems to be that hydroponic can enhance the content of bioactive compounds. Recent studies have shown that in some high-value fresh vegetables, the hydroponic systems allow having higher nutritional quality due to high accumulation of bioactive compounds. Premuzic et al. [36] found an increment of macro- and micronutrients as well as in antioxidants in hydroponic tomatoes, compared to soil-based production. Selma et al. [37] found that hydroponic system was more effective in controlling microbial contamination as well as higher antioxidant compounds, since this method of production allowed a better maintenance of visual quality, control of browning, and more effective in controlling microbial contamination as compared with lettuces cultivated in soil. Pedneault et al. [38] in *Achillea millefolium* found an accumulation of flavonoids in plants grown in hydroponic systems (0.43% dry weigh) compared to field-grown plants 0.38% dry weight). Also, Sgherri et al. [3] found that hydroponic cultivation of basil (*Ocimum basilicum* cv. Genova) improved the antioxidant activity of both aqueous and lipid extracts, increasing the contents of vitamin C, vitamin E, lipoic acid, total phenols, and rosmarinic acid. **Table 3** presents some examples of studies about the accumulation of bioactive compounds under hydroponic systems.

Based on the results obtained by the different authors, it seems evident that all of them reported as common reasons for the enhancement of bioactive compounds under hydroponics—the tight control over the entire process of cultivation, particularly the amount and composition of nutrients and environmental conditions of temperature, humidity and light, and water salinity. Hydroponic operations, including the water recirculation systems, may provide ideal conditions for enactment of secondary metabolites, particularly when plants are placed under osmotic or salt stress, which boost the natural bioactive compounds of plants. Moreover, the saturation of light and temperatures by leaf receptors, often used in these systems, contributes

Crop	Results	Reference
Basil	The hydroponic cultivation improved the contents of vitamin C, vitamin E, lipoic acid, total phenols, and rosmarinic acid, as well as their antioxidant activities.	[3]
Lettuce	Hydroponics offered 11 ± 1.7 times higher yields compared to conventionally produced, but also required 82 ± 11 times more energy.	[4]
Lettuce	Levels of alpha-tocopherol here were higher in hydroponics compared to conventional soil-based production.	[5]
Lettuce	The content of lutein, beta-carotene, violaxanthin, and neoxanthin were lower in hydroponics compared to the soil-based production, due to less exposure of hydroponics to sunlight and temperatures, which had significant impact on carotenogenesis decreasing their levels.	[6]
Lettuce	Hydroponics-grown lettuce had significantly lower concentration of microorganisms compared to other in-soil-grown lettuce.	[7]
Onion	Total flavonoids were similar between hydroponics and soil-based cultivation.	[8]
Red paprika	The content of carotenoids capsorubin and capsanthin was higher in hydroponics (4.50 and 46.74 mg/100 g dry weight, respectively) compared to convention soil culture (2.81 and 29.57 mg/100 g dry weight, respectively).	[9]
Strawberry	Fruit yield per plant was 10% higher in hydroponic raspberries compared to soil-grown raspberries.	[10]
Sweet potato	Carotenes, ascorbic acid, thiamin, oxalic and tannic acids, and chymotrypsin and trypsin inhibitors were higher under hydroponics.	[11]
Tomato	No significant differences between hydroponic and nonhydroponic tomatoes in the levels of lycopene content (averaging 36.15 and 36.25 μg/g, respectively).	[11]
Tomato	Highly controlled conditions of electrical conductivity (EC) and salinity of water, pH, and nutrients provide optimum condition for enhancing the levels of sugars, Brix, pH, and organic acids, which are quality criteria of consumer acceptance toward tomato.	[12]

Table 3. Comparative results between hydroponics and conventional soil-based production.

to maximize photosynthesis and subsequent carbohydrate production that will be used for different biochemical mechanism including bioactive compounds biosynthesis, enhancing their content. For example, Greer and Weston [39] found that in a controlled environment with lower temperatures, the content of anthocyanin in berries increased. Other authors observed an increment of phenolic acids, flavonoids, and anthocyanins when the ratio of day/night temperature and day/night length was modified from low to high [40]. Also, in a recent study [41] with rocket salads (*Eruca sativa, Eruca vesicaria,* and *Diplotaxis tenuifolia*), it was found that setting long day lighting (16 h light, 8 h dark) at an intensity of 200 μmol m^{-2} s^{-1}, with a daytime temperatures of 20°C and night-time temperatures of 14°C, caused an enhancement in the content of polyphenols and glucosinolates. Likewise, day/night temperatures and day/night length, the nutrient solutions, the type of lights, and the levels of CO_2 can be used to enhance the content of bioactive compounds. Nutrient solutions with high electrical conductivity (EC) were shown to be efficient in the increment of lycopene (from 34 to 85%) in tomato cultivars [42]. In a study with *Gynura bicolor* DC (a traditional vegetable from China and South East Asia) submitted to 80% red light and 20% blue light, supplemented with CO_2 elevation from 450 (ambient reading) to 1200 μmol mol^{-1}, the content of bioactive compounds enhanced significantly [43]. The content of anthocyanins and flavonoids rose from 400 to 700 mg 100 g^{-1} dry weight and from 250 to 350 mg 100 g^{-1} dry weight, respectively [43]. Therefore, growing plants in a highly controlled environment might be an efficient alternative to maximize the production of bioactive compounds.

Although there are many advantages of the hydroponics compared to soil-based production, there are several aspects to be taken in account when we decide to choose hydroponics. These types of production systems require a regular irrigation and fertilization, which may otherwise result in possible contamination of surface and groundwater. In addition, they required an adequate management of pH, electrical conductivity (EC), dissolved oxygen, and temperature of nutrient solutions, because the ion concentrations may change with time, resulting in a nutrient imbalance. Therefore, real-time and periodical measurements of nutrient solutions are required, and adjustment of nutrient ratios is often required. In addition, to avoid infestations and diseases, disinfection systems are obligatory. All these aspects must be considered to achieve high quality without compromising the production yield and safety.

3. Conclusions

Hydroponics is extending worldwide and such systems offer many new alternatives and opportunities for growers and consumers to have productions with high quality, including vegetables enhanced with bioactive compounds. This chapter presented a general overview about the role of hydroponics in the enhancement of these important types of nonessential nutrients, and based on the above discussion, it seems that hydroponics can be an essential instrument to have vegetables with high nutritional quality. However, both hydroponics and soil-based production systems require proper control, and they must be implemented correctly with full respect with plant needs, soil, water, environment, growers, and consumer safety.

Acknowledgements

The author acknowledges the support of European Investment Funds by FEDER/COMPETE/POCI–Operational Competitiveness and Internationalization Programme, under Project POCI-01-0145-FEDER-006958 and National Funds by FCT—Portuguese Foundation for Science and Technology, under the project UID/AGR/04033/2013.

Conflict of interest

The author declares no conflict of interest.

References

[1] Kris-Etherton PM, Hecker KD, Bonanome A, Coval SM, Binkoski AE, Hilpert KF, Griel AE, Etherton TD. Bioactive compounds in foods: Their role in the prevention of cardiovascular disease and cancer. The American Journal of Medicine. 2002;**113**:71-88. DOI: 10.1016/S0002-9343(01)00995-0

[2] Biesalski H-K, Dragsted LO, Elmadfa I, Grossklaus R, Müller M, Chrenk D, Walter P, Weber P. Bioactive compounds: Definition and assessment of activity. Nutrition. 2009;**25**:1202-1205. DOI: 10.1016/j.nut.2009.04.023

[3] Sgherri C, Cecconami S, Pinzino C, Navari-Izzo F, Izzo R. Levels of antioxidants and nutraceuticals in basil grown in hydroponics and soil. Food Chemistry. 2010;**123**:416-422. DOI: 10.1016/j.foodchem.2010.04.058

[4] Barbosa GL, Gadelha FDA, Kublik N, Proctor A, Reichelm L, Weissinger E, Wohlleb GM, Halden RU. Comparison of land, water, and energy requirements of lettuce grown using hydroponic vs. conventional agricultural methods. International Journal of Environmental Research and Public Health. 2015;**12**:6879-6891. DOI: 10.3390/ijerph120606879

[5] Buchanan DN, Omaye ST. Comparative study of ascorbic acid and tocopherol concentrations in hydroponic- and soil-grown lettuces. Food and Nutrition Sciences. 2013;**4**:1047-1053. DOI: 10.4236/fns.2013.410136

[6] Kimura M, Rodriguez-Amaya DB. Carotenoid composition of hydroponic leafy vegetables. Journal of Agricultural and Food Chemistry. 2003;**51**:2603-2607. DOI: 10.1021/jf020539b

[7] Sirsat SA, Neal JA. Microbial profile of soil-free versus in-soil grown lettuce and intervention methodologies to combat pathogen surrogates and spoilage microorganisms on lettuce. Food. 2013;**2**:488-498. DOI: 10.3390/foods2040488

[8] Thompson L, Morris J, Peffley E, Green C, Paré P, Tissue D, Jasoni R, Hutson J, Wehner B, Kane C. Flavonol content and composition of spring onions grown hydroponically or in potting soil. Journal of Food Composition and Analysis. 2005;**18**:635-645. DOI: 10.1016/j.jfca.2004.06.009

[9] Kim J-S, An CG, Park J-S, Lim YP, Kim S. Carotenoid profiling from 27 types of paprika (*Capsicum annuum* L.) with different colors, shapes, and cultivation methods. Food Chemistry. 2016;**201**:64-71. DOI: 10.1016/j.foodchem.2016.01.041

[10] Treftz C, Omaye ST. Nutrient analysis of soil and soilless strawberries and raspberries grown in a greenhouse. Food and Nutrition Sciences. 2015;**6**:805-815. DOI: 10.4236/fns.2015.69084

[11] Ajlouni S, Kremer S, Masih L. Lycopene content in hydroponic and non-hydroponic tomatoes during postharvest storage. Food Australia. 2001;**53**:195-196. https://www.researchgate.net/profile/Said:Ajlouni/publication/259198470_Lycopene_content_in_hydroponic_and_non-hydroponic_tomatoes_during_postharvest_storage/links/53d9cca90cf2631430c7dc55.pdf [Accessed: November 23, 2017]

[12] DeBoer B. Tasty Tomatoes: Improving Flavor and Quality in Hydroponically Grown Tomatoes. 2016. Available from: https://www.maximumyield.com/tasty-tomatoes-improving-flavor-and-quality-in-hydroponically-grown-tomatoes/2/1073 [Accessed: November 22, 2017]

[13] Savvas D. Hydroponics: A modern technology supporting the application of integrated crop management in greenhouse. Food, Agriculture & Environment. 2003;**1**:80-86. https://pdfs.semanticscholar.org/b334/0b0d3ac38b219eac05e3390dc680f0d47741.pdf [Accessed: 17 November 2017]

[14] Douglas JS. Hydroponics. 5th ed. Bombay: Oxford; 1975. pp. 1-3

[15] Jensen MH, Collins WL. Hydroponic vegetable production. Horticultural Reviews. 1985;**7**:483-558. DOI: 10.1002/9781118060735.ch10

[16] Hughes AJ. Experts: Hydroponic Growing Offers Advantages, But Won't Replace the Soil. 2017. Available from: http://seedstock.com/2016/03/15/experts-hydroponic-growing-offers-advantages-but-wont-replace-soil/ [Accessed: 20 November 2017]

[17] Sarah Wambua S. Reasons Why Hydroponics Is Better Than Soil Farming. 2017. Available from: http://www.farmhydroponics.com/hydroponics/hydroponics-vs-soil [Accessed: November 20, 2017]

[18] Okemwa E. Effectiveness of aquaponic and hydroponic gardening to traditional gardening. International Journal of Scientific Research and Innovative Technology. 2015;**2**:2313-3759. http://www.ijsrit.com/uploaded_all_files/3563230518_m3.pdf [Accessed: November 20, 2017]

[19] Nguyen NT, McInturf SA, Mendoza-Cózatl DG. Hydroponics: A versatile system to study nutrient allocation and plant responses to nutrient availability and exposure to toxic elements. Journal of Visualized Experiments. 2016;**113**:54317. DOI: 10.3791/54317

[20] Lopes da Luz G, Petter Medeiros S, Manfron P, Borcioni E, Muller L, Dischkaln do Amaral A, Pereira Morais K. Consumo de energia elétrica e produção de alface hidropônica com três intervalos entre irrigações. Ciência Rural. 2008;**38**:815-818. DOI: 10.1590/S0103-84782008000800049

[21] Mehra S, Leng TW, Yamashita Y. Are Singaporeans Ready for Hydroponics? 2017. Available from: http://www.aci-institute.com/wp-content/uploads/2017/08/Insight-_Singaporeans_hydroponics_Shyamli_WeeLeng_Yuko.pdf [Accessed: November 20, 2017]

[22] Treftz C, Omaye ST. Hydroponics: Potential for augmenting sustainable food production in non-arable regions. Nutrition & Food Science. 2016;**46**:672-684. DOI: 10.1108/NFS-10-2015-0118

[23] Horrigan L, Lawrence RS, Walker P. How sustainable agriculture can address the environmental and human health harms of industrial agriculture. Environmental Health Perspectives. 2002;**110**:445-456. https://www.ncbi.nlm.nih.gov/pmc/articles/PMC1240832/ [Accessed: November 20, 2017]

[24] Bridgewood L. Hydroponics: Soilless Gardening Explained. Marlborough: Crowood Press; 2003. p. 144. ISBN 9781861265609

[25] Jones JB Jr. Hydroponics: A Practical Guide for the Soilless Grower. 2nd ed. CRC Press; 2005. p. 440. ISBN: 1420037706, 9781420037708

[26] Resh HM. Hydroponic Food Production: A Definitive Guidebook for the Advanced Home Gardener and the Commercial Hydroponic Grower. 7th ed. CRC Press; 2012. p. 560. ISBN 9781439878675

[27] Hughes C. The 6 Most Common Types of Hydroponic Systems Found in Modern Grow Rooms. 2017. Available from: https://www.maximumyield.com/the-6-most-common-types-of-hydroponic-systems-found-in-modern-grow-rooms/2/3614 [Accessed: November 20, 2017]

[28] Lennard WA, Leonard BV. A comparison of three different hydroponic sub-systems (gravel bed, floating and nutrient film technique) in an aquaponic test system. Aquacult International. 2006;**14**:539-550. DOI: 10.1007/s10499-006-9053-2

[29] Halliwell B. Dietary polyphenols: Good, bad, or indifferent for your health? Cardiovascular Research. 2007;**73**:341-347. DOI: 10.1016/j.cardiores.2006.10.004

[30] Kris-Etherton PM, Hecker KD, Bonanome A, Coval SM, Binkosky AE, Hilpert KF, Griel AE, Etherton DT. Bioactive compounds in foods: Their role in the prevention of cardiovascular disease and cancer. The American Journal of Medicine. 2002;**113**(Suppl. 9B):71-88S. DOI: 10.1016/S0002-9343(01)00995-0

[31] Delgoda R, Murray JE. Evolutionary perspectives on the role of plant secondary metabolites. In: Badal S, Delgoda R, editors. Pharmacognosy. Boston: Academic Press; 2017. pp. 93-100. DOI: 10.1016/B978-0-12-802104-0.00007-X

[32] Maboko MM, Du Plooy CP, Bertling I. Comparative performance of tomato cultivars in soilless vs. in-soil production systems. Acta Horticulturae. 2009;**843**:319-326. DOI: 10.17660/ActaHortic.2009.843.42

[33] Palermo M, Paradiso R, De Pascale S, Fogliano V. Hydroponic cultivation improves the nutritional quality of soybean and its products. Journal of Agricultural and Food Chemistry. 2012;**60**:250-255. DOI: 10.1021/jf203275m

[34] Rouphael Y, Colla G. Growth, yield, fruit quality and nutrient uptake of hydroponically cultivated zucchini squash as affected by irrigation systems and growing seasons. Science and Horticulture. 2005;**105**:177-195. DOI: 10.1016/j.scienta.2005.01.025

[35] Murphy MT, Zhang F, Nakamura YK, Omaye ST. Comparison between hydroponically and conventionally and organically grown lettuces for taste, odor, visual quality and texture: A pilot study. Food and Nutrition Sciences. 2011;**2**:124-127. DOI: 10.4236/fns.2011.22017

[36] Premuzic Z, Bargiela M, Garcia A, Rendina A, Iorio A. Calcium, iron, potassium, phosphorus, and vitamin C content of organic and hydroponic tomatoes. HortScience. 1998;**33**:255-225

[37] Selma MV, Luna MC, Martínez-Sánchez A, Tudela JÁ, Beltrán D, Baixauli C, Gil MI. Sensory quality, bioactive constituents and microbiological quality of green and red fresh-cut lettuces (*Lactuca sativa* L.) are influenced by soil and soilless agricultural production systems. Postharvest Biology and Technology. 2012;**63**:16-24. DOI: 10.1016/j.postharvbio.2011.08.002

[38] Pedneault K, Léonhart S, Gosselin A, Papadopoulos AP, Dorais M, Angers P. Variations in concentration of active compounds in four hydroponically and field-grown medicinal plant species. Acta Horticulturae. 2002;**580**:255-262. DOI: 10.17660/ActaHortic.2002.580.34

[39] Greer DH, Weston C. Heat stress affects flowering, berry growth, sugar accumulation and photosynthesis of *Vitis vinifera* cv. *Semillon* grapevines grown in a controlled environment. Functional Plant Biology. 2010;**37**:206-214. DOI: 10.1071/FP09209

[40] Shashirekha MN, Mallikarjuna SE, Rajarathnam S. Status of bioactive compounds in foods, with focus on fruits and vegetables. Critical Reviews in Food Science and Nutrition. 2015;**55**:1324-1339. DOI: 10.1080/10408398.2012.692736

[41] Almazan AM, Begum F, Jonson C. Nutritional quality of sweetpotato greens from greenhouse plants. Journal of Food Composition and Analysis. 1997;**10**:246-253. DOI: 10.1006/jfca.1997.0538

[42] Kubota C, Thomson CA, Wu M, Javanmardi J. Controlled environments for production of value-added food crops with high phytochemical concentrations: Lycopene in tomato as an example. HortScience. 2006;**41**:522-525. http://hortsci.ashspublications.org/content/41/3/522.abstract

[43] Ren J, Guo S-S, Xin X-L, Chen L. Changes in volatile constituents and phenols from *Gynura bicolor* DC grown in elevated CO_2 and LED lighting. Science and Horticulture. 2014;**175**:243-250. DOI: 10.1016/j.scienta.2014.06.023

Chapter 5

The Influence of Different Substrates on the Growth, Yield and Quality of Slovenian Sweetpotato Cultivars under Greenhouse Conditions

Abstract

A greenhouse experiment was conducted to evaluate the genetic relatedness between three Slovenian sweetpotato cultivars; and to assess the effects of different growing substrates on selected agronomic and nutritional traits. Tubers of three cultivars ('Lučka', 'Janja' and 'Martina') with different skin/flesh color were produced in planters under glasshouse conditions in five different growing substrates (perlite, peat, expanded clay, vermiculite and garden soil) from prior raised seedlings. Genetic analysis was performed using a set of eight SSR markers. According to Nei's genetic distance and pairwise population Fst analysis, the most related cultivars are 'Janja' and 'Martina'. The following agronomic traits were evaluated: vine length, thickness of vine-base, number of branches, weight of above ground part, number of leaves plant^{-1}, number of tubers plant^{-1} and tubers weight plant^{-1}. Among nutritional traits, total phenolic content (TPC), antioxidant potential (AOP) and ascorbic acid content (AA) were determined. Significant interactions of growing substrates (factor A) × cultivar (factor B) were observed for thickness of vine-base, weight of above ground part, AOP, TPC and AA. Overall results show different response of cultivars in different growing substrate. Growing substrate provide a discriminant classification of the sweetpotato cultivars according to their agronomic and nutritional traits.

Keywords: growing substrates, genetic analysis, *Ipomoea batatas*, phenolic compounds

1. Introduction

The sweetpotato (*Ipomoea batatas* Lam.) is an herbaceous dicotyledonous perennial plant grown primarily as a root crop. In systematic plant taxonomy, the sweetpotato is assigned to the family Convolvulaceae Juss., which comprises 55 genera [1]. To distinguish the sweetpotato from the tuberous potato (*Solanum tuberosum* L.), the internationally accepted convention for the common English name is now the one word spelling 'sweetpotato' [2]. Although sweetpotato shoot tips and leaves may be eaten, the swollen root is the main part used for human consumption.

Ranked by current world production, sweetpotato is the 7th major crop, which serves as an energy and phytochemical source of nutrition in more than 100 countries [3]. The origin of sweetpotato is Central America, but at present it is widely cultivated in the tropics and subtropics, and even in some temperate areas at different ecological regions [4]. The main sweetpotato production regions by area include Asia (78.4%), Africa (17.1%), North America (1.8%), South America (1.3%) and Oceania (1.2%). In Europe, where the total production of sweetpotato accounted 45.901 t in 2016, the biggest producers are Portugal (22.591 t), Spain (13.550 t), Italy (6.723 t) and Greece (3.038 t) [5]. In Slovenia, sweetpotato has been quite unknown crop until recently, both for production and human consumption. The environment diversity and specific climatic conditions of this region could enable successful production of that crop in the future [6, 7]. Three new Slovenian sweetpotato cultivars ('Lučka', 'Janja' and 'Martina') were registered in 2015 and are now added to national list of varieties [8]. According of Yamakawa and Yoshimoto [9] of particular importance is the development of novel cultivars with roots contributing to the human diet, both as basic food stuff but with added physiological functions such as antioxidant or specific nutritional traits.

Tubers of sweetpotato are rich in dietary fiber, minerals, vitamins and antioxidants, such as phenolic compounds [10–12]. Besides acting as antioxidants, phenolic compounds and carotenoids also provide sweetpotatoes with their distinctive flesh/skin colors (cream, deep yellow, orange and purple) [13]. Contribution of sweetpotato toward health is acknowledged due to high nutrient content and its anti-carcinogenic and cardiovascular disease preventing properties [4, 14]. In recent years, several reports have indicated that the phytochemicals from sweetpotatoes displayed antioxidative or radical scavenging activity with health-promoting functions [15, 16]. Phenolic acids (i.e., chlorogenic and dicaffeoylquinic acids) contribute to antioxidant activity and other health beneficial properties of color fleshed genotypes [17, 18]. Additionally, cultivars with the same flesh color may differ in total phenolic content, individual phenolic acid profile and antioxidant activity.

Sweetpotato readily produces adventitious roots and has trailing vines, therefore can colonize marginal soils and is not very demanding as regards soil type [19].

The most innovative technology of plant cultivation in greenhouse conditions is growing in mineral substrates. The origin of substrates is different and they also differ in their physical, chemical and biological properties. According to Kacjan Maršić and Jakše [20] peat, perlite, expanded clay and vermiculite are an efficient growing media in the European market. Peat consists of partially decomposed aquatic, marsh, bog or swamp vegetation. The main advantages of peat lie in its physical properties, which allow an adequate water/air ratio in the root zone, and a high cation exchange capacity able to adequately provide nutrient for plant growth and development [21]. Perlite is a substance made from volcanic rock and often used as a soil additive to increase aeration and draining of the soil. It is also relatively inexpensive. The biggest drawback to perlite is that it does not retain water very well. Spain is the pioneer among the Mediterranean countries in the commercial use of perlite, mainly for vegetable production [22]. There are several studies on possibilities of using perlite as a substrate and it has been reported that the average yield of fruit-bearing crops cultivated in perlite achieved 2–3 times higher yield than plants grown in soil [23]. It has been also reported that growers in the Mediterranean region prefer perlite to other substrates because it is easily available from local suppliers, it is cheap and can be used for at least three, instead of 2 years, which is the common maximum durability of most other substrates. Expanded clay pellets are made by baking clay in a kiln. Clay pellets are full of tiny air pockets, which give them good drainage. They are best for systems that have frequent watering. Because expanded clay pellets do not have good water-holding capacity, salt accumulation and drying out can be common problems in improperly managed systems. Although the pellets are rather expensive, they are one of the few kinds of medium that can be easily reused [24]. Vermiculite is a micaceous mineral which is expanded when heated in furnaces at temperatures near 109°C. Chemically, it is a hydrated magnesium-aluminum-iron silicate. When expanded, it is very light in weight (96–160 kg/m^3) and neutral in reaction with good buffering properties. It is able to absorb large quantities of water (0.4–0.5 m/cm^3). It has a relatively high cation exchange capacity and thus can hold nutrients in reserve and later release them. It contains some magnesium and potassium which is available to plants [25].

The required physical and chemical characteristics of growth substrates vary notably with crop species and its management, and substrate choice can be influenced by environmental and economic considerations [26]. Afterward, growing substrates are easier to handle and it may provide better growing environment compared to soil culture [27, 28]. To the best of our knowledge, there is no scientific literature regarding cultivation of sweetpotato in different growing substrates.

Application of short sequence repeats (SSR) markers in genetic diversity studies of different agro-economically important species represents informative, effective and reliable marker system [29–34] for distinguishing between different genetic resources. For sweetpotato, which is a hexaploid (2n = 6x = 90) plant species with an out-crossing mating system [35], SSR marker system is highly applicable due its codominant nature [32].

The objective of the study was to analyze the genetic relatedness between three Slovenian sweetpotato cultivars, to examine the effect of different growing substrates on selected agronomic and nutritional traits of these cultivars and to compare responses between cultivars.

2. Materials and methods

2.1. Experimental setup

The experiment was carried out at the Glasshouse experimental station (46°04'N, 14°31'W; altitude 310 m a.s.l.) of the Biotechnical Faculty in Ljubljana, Slovenia. Three new Slovenian cultivars of sweetpotato (*Ipomoea batatas* L.) were studied: 'Lučka' with orange skin and flesh color, 'Janja' with white skin and flesh color and 'Martina' purple skin and white flesh color (**Figures 1** and **2**). **Table 1** shows the main characteristics of cultivars.

Cuttings and seedlings were grown in styrofoam seed starting trays filled with substrate for seedlings Neuhaus N3 (Humko, Slovenia) and covered with vermiculite.

Polypropylene troughs (Mapal Plastic Agricultural Products Division, Israel) were placed on parallel beds. Each of three troughs—blocks (18 m length, 0.5 m width and 0.2 m height) was divided to plots, separated with polystyrene dams to avoid stirring and filled with growing media. In each plot two seedlings of individual cultivar were planted. The randomized complete block design (RCBD) was split plot with growing media applied to whole plots and cultivars applied to split plots. The experiment was designed to test two factors: different growing substrates (factor A; perlite, peat, expanded clay, vermiculite and garden soil) and different sweetpotato cultivars (factor B).

After the initial watering of the substrate and seedlings, T-tape tubes (T-Tape® TSX 500 Model) were placed over the growing substrate. Basic fertilization was performed with water soluble NPK fertilizer Entec Perfect (14-7-17, EuroChem Agro, Germany; 350 kg ha^{-1}) during planting of seedlings in growing substrate in the beginning of June. Two weeks after transplantation and throughout the growing period, the plants were fertilized three times per week with

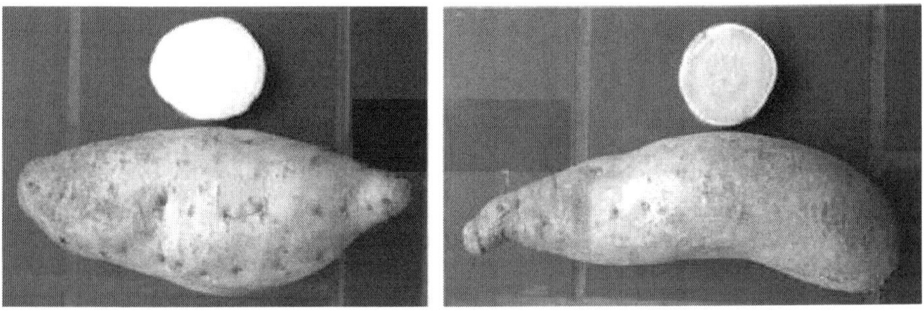

Figure 1. Cv. 'Janja' (left) and cv. 'Lučka' (right) (photo: D. Žnidarčič).

Figure 2. Cv. 'Martina' (photo: D. Žnidarčič).

Characteristics	Cultivar					
	'Lučka'		'Janja'		'Martina'	
	State of expression	**Note**	**State of expression**	**Note**	**State of expression**	**Note**
Plant growth habit	Spreading	5	Spreading	5	Spreading	5
Length of primary shoots	Medium	5	Short	3	Short	3
Length of internode	Medium	5	Medium	5	Medium	5
Diameter of internode	Medium	5	Medium	5	Very large	9
Anthocyanin coloration of internode	Absent or week	1	Absent or week	1	Absent or week	1
Anthocyanin coloration of tip	Medium	2	Absent or week	1	Absent or week	1
Anthocyanin coloration of node	Medium	2	Absent or week	1	Absent or week	1
Pubescens of tip	Absent or sparse	1	Absent or sparse	1	Dense	3
Leaf blade: lobes	Absent	1	Three lobes	2	Absent	1
Leaf blade: shape	Triangular	2	Triangular	2	Triangular	2
Leaf blade: depth of lobing	—	—	Very shallow	1	—	—
Leaf blade: color	Green	2	Green	2	Green	2
Leaf blade: anthocyanin coloration of upper side	Absent or week	1	Absent or week	1	Absent or week	1
Leaf blade: extent of anthocyanin coloration on abaxial veins	Small	3	Absent or very small	1	Absent or very small	1
Leaf blade: intensity of anthocyanin coloration on abaxial veins	Weak	3	Very weak	1	Very weak	1
Young leaf blade: main color on upper side	Purplish brown	7	Medium green	3	Medium green	3
Petiole: anthocyanin coloration	Absent or very week	1	Absent or very week	1	Absent or very week	1
Petiole: length	Short	3	Short	3	Short	3
Storage root: shape	Ovate	1	Ovate	1	Ovate	1
Storage root: ratio length/width	Medium	5	Moderately elongated	7	Medium	5
Storage root: thickness of cortex relative to overall diameter	Thick	7	Thick	7	Medium	5
Storage root: main color of skin	Brownish orange	5	Light beige	2	Light purple	9
Storage root: secondary color of skin	Brown	8	Pink	5	Pink	5
Storage root: main color of flesh	Orange	4	Beige	2	Beige	2

Characteristics	Cultivar					
	'Lučka'		'Janja'		'Martina'	
	State of expression	Note	State of expression	Note	State of expression	Note
Storage root: intensity main color of flesh	Medium	2	Light	1	Light	1
Storage root: secondary color of flesh	Yellow	3	Yellow	3	White	1
Storage root: depth of eyes	Shallow	1	Shallow	1	Shallow	1

Table 1. Characteristics of sweetpotato cultivars (included in the UPOV test guidelines, CPVO technical protocol or reporting authority's test guidelines).

nutrient solution prepared with tap water-containing water soluble NPK fertilizer Polifid (16-8-32, Haifa, Israel; 1 g L^{-1}). During the growth period the following measures were implemented: removing weeds, monitoring the functioning of the irrigation system, cleaning dead plant parts and monitoring the presence of pests and diseases.

At harvest, after 128 days growing period, the following agronomic traits (growth and yield parameters) were evaluated for individual cultivar and growing substrate: vine length (cm), thickness of vine-base (mm), number of branches, weight of above ground part (g), number of leaves ($plant^{-1}$), number of tubers ($plant^{-1}$) and tubers weight (kg $plant^{-1}$). The proximate analysis of the tubers was also assessed. For the analysis of total phenolic content (TPC), antioxidant potential (AOP) and ascorbic acid content (AA), random tubers of each cultivar and growing substrate were used. For the sample extraction, 8 g of fresh tuber slices (flesh and skin) were mixed with 10 g of 2% metaphosphoric acid dissolved in distilled water. The tissue was homogenized using an Ultraturax T 25 (20,500 rpm). Homogenized samples were centrifuged and filtered through a 0.45 μm filters (17 mm syringe filter CA). The extracts were stored at −80°C until analyzed.

2.2. Genetic analysis

Genomic DNA was extracted from frozen leaves of six different plants collected individually from each of three cultivars grown in garden soil. BioSprint 15 DNA Plant Kit (Qiagen, Germany) and MagMax (Applied Biosystems, USA) nucleic acids isolation robot, following the modified method from manufacturer's instructions, were used. Dilutions of 1 ng μL^{-1} of DNA were used for PCR amplification. Eight primer pairs: Ib-316, Ib-318, Ib-242, Ib-248, Ib-255F1, Ib-255, Ib-286 and Ib-297 [35, 36] were applied for SSR assessment. PCR reactions were performed in a final volume of 11 μL, containing 1 ng of genomic DNA and following reagents with starting concentrations of: 10× PCR buffer (Biotools, Spain), 10 mM of each dNTP's, 50 mM $MgCl_2$ (Biotools, Spain), 10 μM of each primer, 10 μM 5′ fluorescently labeled universal primer (6-FAM, NED and HEX) and 0.5 U of Taq DNA polymerase (Biotools, Spain). The forward primer of each SSR was appended with 18 bp tail sequence 5′-TGTAAAACGACGGCCAGT-3′ (M13(−21)) as described by Schuelke [37]. PCR analyses were performed on ABI 9700 (Applied Biosystems, USA) under the following 'touch-down' conditions: 94°C for 4 min, 30 cycles at

94°C for 1 min, auto increment temperature from 49.5°C for 0.5°C per cycle for 30 s, 72°C for 1 min, followed by 30 cycles at 94°C for 30 s, auto increment temperature from 49.5°C for 0.5°C per cycle for 30 s, 72°C for 1 min and final extension for 5 min at 72°C. Fragment analysis was performed on 3130XL Genetic Analyzer (Applied Biosystems, USA), the allele lengths were determined by comparison with size standard GeneScan-350 ROX (Applied Biosystems, USA) using GeneMapper 4.0 (Applied Biosystems, USA). Parameters of genetic diversity among loci and varieties, including number of migrants (Nm), inbreeding coefficients (Fst), % of polymorphic loci, numbers of effective alleles, total expected heterozygosities (Ht), Shannon's information index, pairwise Nei's genetic correlations, pairwise population Fst analysis, analysis of molecular variance via R-statistics under 999 permutations (AMOVA) and principal coordinate analysis (PCoA) were conducted applying GenAlEx v.6.4 [38].

2.3. Analysis of nutritional traits

Analyses of bioactive compounds included evaluation of TPC, AOP and AA in tubers of sweetpotato. The TPC was determined using the Folin-Ciocalteu method, as described by Singleton and Rossi, and slightly modified [39]. Gallic acid (Merck, Germany) was used for six point calibration curve, which ranged from 3 to 150 mg L^{-1} ($R^2 = 0.9998$). The results were expressed as gallic acid equivalents (mg GAE 100 g^{-1} FW; fresh weight). The AOP was evaluated using the DPPH (2,2-diphenyl-1-picrylhydrazyl; Sigma-Aldrich, Saint Louis, MO, USA) free radical scavenging method [40]. Trolox (220 mg L^{-1}; Sigma-Aldrich, Saint Louis, MO, USA) was used for six point calibration curve, which ranged from 40 to 220 mg L^{-1} ($R^2 = 0.9900$). The results were expressed as Trolox equivalents (mg TE g^{-1} FW). AA analysis was performed on an HPLC system (Agilent 1260; Agilent Technologies) using a diode array detector, with the wavelength set at 254 nm. The determination of AA was carried out on a 100 × 2 mm i.d., 3 μm Scherzo SM-C18 column (Imtakt, Japan), at a flow rate of 0.3 mL min^{-1}. The mobile phase consisted of water (A) and acetonitrile (B), both of which contained 0.3% formic acid. The following elution gradient was used for solvent B: 0–3 min, 0–10%; 3–4 min, 10–100% and 4–6 min, 100%. The temperature of the column was maintained at 30°C, while the temperature of the automatic sample feeder was set at 4°C. AA was calculated using an external standard method and expressed as mg 100 g^{-1} FW.

2.4. Statistical analyses

Statistical analyses were performed using the Centurion Statgraphics XVI statistical analysis program. Prior statistical analyses data was tested for normal distribution using Shapiro-Wilk test. If the data were not normally distributed, log transformation was used prior further analysis. For easier interpretation the **Tables 3** and **4** show the untransformed data. Multifactorial ANOVA analysis was used to determine statistical significance of main factors and interaction of sweetpotato varieties with the growing media. The model was specified in GLM according to split plot experimental design. When ANOVA showed statistical significances, means were separated using Tukey's HSD test ($P < 0.05$). Multivariate analysis was carried out using the XLSTAT software package. For determination of key traits responsible for discrimination based on differences in growing media for all sweetpotato samples and differences according to sweetpotato variety, the multivariate analysis by discriminant analysis was used.

3. Results and discussion

3.1. Genetic differentiation

SSR screening of sweetpotato cultivars was performed on eight loci (91.7% polymorphic loci) where the highest levels (Ht > 0.65) of genetic differentiation were assigned to loci Ib-318, Ib-297, Ib-248, Ib-242 and Ib-286. Locus Ib-255 reflected the lowest informativity through low Ht (0.278), high inbreeding coefficient (Fst = 0.400) and the lowest number of genetic migrants (Nm = 0.375), detected among genotypes. According to parameters of genetic diversity for specific loci, described in **Table 2**, the most effective genetic differentiation was obtained for locus Ib-286, where the lowest proportion of total genetic diversity that separates cultivars was calculated via Fst (0.082) and the highest number of genetic migrants among genotypes and cultivars (Nm = 2.813) was detected.

	'Janja'	'Martina'	'Lučka'
'Janja'	*	0.072	0.148
'Martina'	0.829	*	0.153
'Lučka'	0.626	0.608	*

Table 2. Pairwise population comparisons of Nei genetic identity (below diagonal) and pairwise population Fst values (above diagonal).

AMOVA was performed through R-statistics ($P \geq 0.01$), where Rst is an estimator of genetic differentiation for SSR loci that assumes a stepwise mutation model. Therefore, molecular variance among varieties was 36%, among genotypes 63% and within genotypes 1%, respectively. In contrast, report about evaluation of genetic variability of sweetpotato germplasm, originated from Africa, Asia and USA shows only 23% of genetic variance between different accessions [41]. Therefore, our study indicate the low level of genetic relatedness between cultivars 'Lučka', 'Janja' and 'Martina' compared to the genetic relatedness between different genetic resources from geographically distant genetic origins. First three axes in PCoA cumulatively explain 76.2% of genetic variation within observed genotypes and cultivars (data not shown). Allelic patterns across three sweetpotato varieties (**Figure 3**) showed that the most genetically diverse variety is 'Martina'. Meanwhile, variety 'Lučka' possess the highest number of alleles which are unique and specific for this variety only.

According to Nei's genetic distance and pairwise population Fst analysis, the most related cultivars are 'Janja' and 'Martina'; in contrast, 'Lučka' and 'Martina' show the weakest genetic linkages (**Table 2**).

3.2. Growth, yield and nutritional parameters

Table 3 shows the summary statistics of main factors and interactions and **Table 4** shows the effect of different growing substrate and cultivar on agronomic and nutritional traits

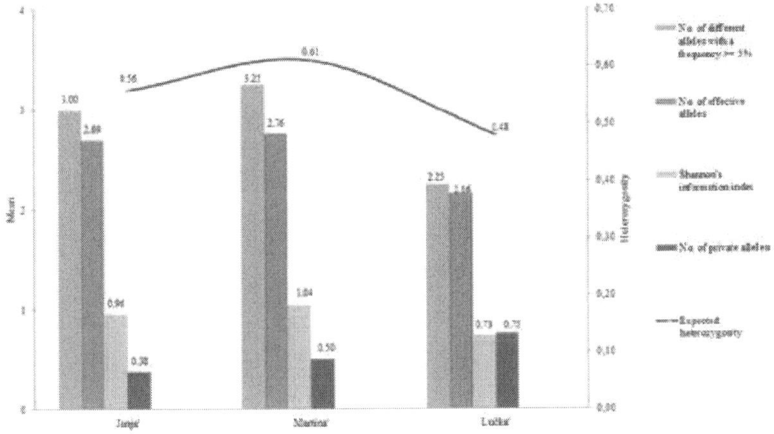

Figure 3. Allelic patterns according to genetic analysis across observed sweetpotato cultivars.

of sweetpotato. Measurements of agronomic traits showed that among growing substrate (factor A) vermiculite had the greatest impact on the vine length (144.4 cm). Between sweetpotato cultivars (factor B), significantly longer vine length was observed for 'Lučka' (147.1 cm). For thickness of vine-base significant differences were found for factor growing substrate, but not for cultivar. The thickness of vine-base (10.7 mm) was significantly higher in expanded clay. Number of branches was significantly higher for sweetpotato grown in peat (13.0), while between cultivars 'Martina' (10.9) and 'Janja' (10.6) had significantly more branches than 'Lučka'. Both, growing substrate and cultivar, had significant impact on weight of above ground part. The weight of above ground part was significantly higher for sweetpotato grown in peat (1402.4 g). Cultivar 'Martina' produced significantly higher weight of above ground part (1177.5 g), that is, more than double as 'Lučka' (463.7 g). Significantly higher number of leaves plant^{-1} was observed for 'Martina' (113.1), and between growing substrate in peat (131.1) and perlite (123.9). Both yield components, number of tubers plant^{-1} and tubers weight plant^{-1} were the lowest for sweetpotatoes grown in garden soil. Comparison between cultivars showed that 'Janja' had the highest yield. Mukhtar et al. [19] reported similar findings for vine length, number of branches and number of leaves plant^{-1} when tested two local sweetpotato cultivars with orange and white flesh.

Analyses of nutritional traits included TPC, AOP and AA of tubers. Data showed significant differences ($P \leq 0.001$) between the growing substrate and the cultivars in all three traits (**Table 3**). The TPC ranged from 36.2 to 65.1 mg GAE 100 g^{-1} FW, AOP from 0.18 to 0.56 mg TE g^{-1} FW and AA from 13.7 to 23.5 mg 100 g^{-1} FW (**Table 4**). Significantly lower TPC was determined in peat (41.2 mg GAE 100 g^{-1} FW). Between cultivars significantly higher TPC was observed in 'Lučka' (60.1 mg GAE 100 g^{-1} FW). Cultivar 'Lučka' with orange flesh color showed significantly higher TPC compared to the other two white flesh colored cultivars, which is in agreement with previous studies on other cultivars [3, 11, 42]. Similar to TPC, higher AOP was found for sweetpotato grown in perlite, expanded clay and vermiculite (for all >0.44 mg TE g^{-1} FW). Tubers of cultivars

	Vine length (cm)	Thickness of vine-base (mm)	Number of branches	Weight of above ground part (g)	Number of leaves plant^{-1}	Number of tubers plant^{-1}	Tubers weight plant^{-1} (g)	TPC (mg GAE 100 g^{-1} FW)	AOP (mg TE g^{-1} FW)	AA (mg 100 g^{-1} FW)
Factor A (growing substrate)										
Perlite	107.3	6.9 c	8.5 ab	724.6 b	123.9 a	15.8 a	982.2 ab	54.1 a	0.50 a	19.7 a
Peat	129.8	9.3 ab	13.0 a	1402.4 a	131.1 a	11.0 a	1517.6 a	41.2 b	0.32 c	16.7 b
Expanded clay	133.8	10.7 a	11.0 ab	934.9 ab	91.1 ab	14.1 a	1198.6 a	54.5 a	0.44 ab	16.6 b
Vermiculite	144.4	9.3 ab	9.9 ab	663.9 b	68.0 b	14.8 a	1358.3 a	53.2 a	0.44 ab	16.2 c
Garden soil	134.1	8.9 b	5.7 b	242.9 c	40.1 c	6.8 b	323.4 b	55.0 a	0.38 bc	16.3 c
P	Ns	**	*	***	***	**	**	***	***	***
Factor B (cultivar)										
'Janja'	119.5 b	9.3	10.6 a	738.0 b	90.6 ab	14.9	1168.0	46.0 c	0.37 b	15.9 b
'Lučka'	147.1 a	8.5	7.6 b	463.7 c	68.9 b	10.1	976.7	60.1 a	0.45 a	20.4 a
'Martina'	123.0 b	9.3	10.9 a	1177.5 a	113.1 a	12.4	1082.3	48.7 b	0.43 a	15.0 c
P	**	Ns	*	***	*	Ns	Ns	***	***	***
Interactions										
A × B	Ns	*	Ns	*	Ns	Ns	Ns	***	***	***

Ns, not significant. Mean values with different letters (a, b, c) in a column are significantly different according to the results of Tukey's HSD test ($P < 0.05$). TPC, total phenolic content; AOP, antioxidant potential; AA, ascorbic acid.

*Level of significance: $P \leq 0.05$.

**Level of significance: $P \leq 0.01$.

***Level of significance: $P \leq 0.001$.

Table 3. Statistics of main factors and interactions for selected agronomic and nutritional traits of sweetpotato.

'Lučka' and 'Martina' had significantly higher AOP, 0.45 and 0.43 mg TE g^{-1} FW, respectively. These results are lower as reported by Tang et al. [11] in their study on different sweetpotato cultivars grown in China. Significantly higher AA was observed in tubers of sweetpotato grown in perlite (19.7 mg 100 g^{-1} FW), while between cultivars significant higher AA was observed in 'Lučka' (20.4 mg 100 g^{-1} FW) (**Table 3**). These data are higher as reported by Suárez et al. [42] on 30 sweetpotato cultivars from Canary Islands, where average values varies from 10 to 14 mg 100 g^{-1} FW.

Significant interactions of growing substrate (factor A) × cultivar (factor B) were observed (**Table 3**) for thickness of vine-base, weight of above ground part, AOP, TPC and AA. Interactions showed that different cultivars showed different response on growing substrate (data not shown). For example, cultivar 'Martina' had significantly higher thickness

Factor A (growing substrate)	Factor B (cultivar)	Vine length (cm)	Thickness of vine-base (mm)	Number of branches	Weight of above ground part (g)	Number of leaves plant^{-1}	Number of tubers plant^{-1}	Tubers weight plant^{-1} (g)	TPC (mg GAE 100 g^{-1} FW)	AOP (mg TE g^{-1} FW)	AA (mg 100 g^{-1} FW)
Perlite	'Lučka'	116.0 ± 22.3	7.0 ± 1.0	6.3 ± 3.5	224.7 ± 42.1	80.7 ± 21.5	13.7 ± 8.0	853.0 ± 497.3	61.3 ± 0.4	0.48 ± 0.07	23.5 ± 1.2
Peat		160.0 ± 21.8	10.3 ± 2.9	11.7 ± 4.6	979.7 ± 235.7	100.0 ± 50.7	9.3 ± 1.5	1279.7 ± 494.7	49.0 ± 7.2	0.35 ± 0.04	20.4 ± 1.0
Expanded clay		144.7 ± 37.1	9.3 ± 1.5	8.3 ± 2.1	483.3 ± 160.6	63.3 ± 15.3	8.3 ± 3.2	1126.7 ± 559.4	65.1 ± 1.1	0.56 ± 0.01	19.6 ± 1.0
Vermiculite		160.3 ± 28.7	9.3 ± 0.6	7.7 ± 2.9	441.0 ± 78.6	61.3 ± 18.6	12.0 ± 2.6	1136.3 ± 512.5	60.5 ± 1.9	0.50 ± 0.03	20.1 ± 1.0
Garden soil		154.7 ± 28.2	6.3 ± 2.3	4.0 ± 0.0	189.7 ± 35.8	39.0 ± 14.4	7.3 ± 1.5	488.0 ± 45.7	64.5 ± 2.4	0.35 ± 0.01	18.5 ± 0.9
Perlite	'Martina'	92.7 ± 4.6	6.7 ± 1.2	10.7 ± 3.5	1205.0 ± 153.9	165.0 ± 59.6	14.7 ± 9.3	1044.3 ± 579.6	52.2 ± 1.3	0.60 ± 0.03	17.2 ± 0.9
Peat		116.7 ± 19.6	7.3 ± 1.2	16.0 ± 2.0	1992.7 ± 238.5	156.7 ± 40.4	12.7 ± 1.2	1639.0 ± 412.7	38.5 ± 1.5	0.18 ± 0.02	14.5 ± 0.7
Expanded clay		136.0 ± 26.9	11.0 ± 2.0	10.3 ± 2.1	1583.3 ± 840.1	131.7 ± 40.7	12.3 ± 1.2	929.7 ± 208.9	49.6 ± 1.6	0.43 ± 0.04	14.4 ± 0.7
Vermiculite		130.3 ± 8.7	9.7 ± 1.5	11.3 ± 2.3	834.7 ± 84.0	73.3 ± 14.4	14.3 ± 5.1	1502.7 ± 763.2	45.6 ± 0.6	0.56 ± 0.03	13.7 ± 0.7
Garden soil		126.5 ± 33.2	11.5 ± 0.7	6.0 ± 0.0	272.0 ± 53.7	38.5 ± 2.1	8.0 ± 5.7	293.5 ± 200.1	57.0 ± 3.8	0.34 ± 0.11	14.7 ± 0.5
Perlite	'Janja'	113.3 ± 15.3	7.0 ± 2.6	8.7 ± 2.1	744.0 ± 271.8	126.0 ± 80.6	19.0 ± 8.7	1049.3 ± 575.4	48.8 ± 2.6	0.43 ± 0.05	18.4 ± 0.9
Peat		112.7 ± 10.8	10.3 ± 3.5	11.3 ± 0.6	1235.0 ± 486.3	136.7 ± 51.1	11.0 ± 4.6	1634.0 ± 957.2	36.2 ± 2.9	0.42 ± 0.03	15.3 ± 0.8
Expanded clay		120.7 ± 9.5	11.7 ± 1.5	14.3 ± 3.1	738.0 ± 162.4	78.3 ± 12.6	21.7 ± 7.4	1539.3 ± 516.7	48.8 ± 1.3	0.32 ± 0.02	15.8 ± 0.8
Vermiculite		142.7 ± 11.0	9.0 ± 2.6	10.7 ± 3.8	716.0 ± 115.9	69.3 ± 12.9	18.0 ± 7.8	1436.0 ± 225.5	53.4 ± 4.4	0.27 ± 0.04	14.9 ± 0.7
Garden soil		108.3 ± 17.6	8.7 ± 1.2	8.0 ± 4.0	267.0 ± 49.8	42.7 ± 10.5	5.0 ± 2.0	181.3 ± 115.6	42.9 ± 0.7	0.43 ± 0.04	15.2 ± 0.8

Data are mean ± standard deviation (n = 3). TPC, total phenolic content; AOP, antioxidant potential; AA, ascorbic acid.

Table 4. Effect of different growing media and cultivar on selected growth, yield and nutritional parameters of sweetpotato.

of vine-base in garden soil, but significantly lowers in peat. However, cultivars 'Janja' and 'Lučka' had significantly higher thickness of vine-base in peat, but significantly lower in garden soil. Cultivar 'Martina' had significantly higher weight of above ground part compared to other cultivars in all growing substrates, except for garden soil. All three cultivars showed significantly higher weight of above ground part in peat. Interactions between cultivars and growing substrate showed significant differences ($P \leq 0.001$) in TPC, AOP and AA. For example, cultivar 'Martina' had significantly higher TPC in tubers grown in garden soil, while cultivar 'Janja' lowers. Cultivar 'Martina' had the lowest AOP in peat, while other cultivars did not show response to this growing substrate. In case of AA all cultivars showed similar response in different growing substrate, except for garden soil.

3.3. Multivariate analyses—discriminant analyses

The discrimination across the original data set of 15 samples originated from 3 sweetpotato cultivars is shown in **Figure 4**. Discriminant analysis was carried out across 10 traits: vine length, thickness of vine-base, number of branches, weight of above ground part, number of leaves plant^{-1}, number of tubers plant^{-1}, tubers weight plant^{-1}, TPC, AOP and AA. The curve defined by the first two discriminant functions (function 1/function 2) represents 100.0% of the total variance for these 10 variables. Function 1 explain 90.7% of the total variance and function 2 9.3% of the total variance. Major contributors to discriminate between different cultivars in function 1 are the AA, number of tubers plant^{-1}, tubers weight plant^{-1} and vine length, respectively; meanwhile the weight of above ground part, TPC, AOP and number of tubers plant^{-1} are major contributors in function 2. The groups of the sweetpotato culti-

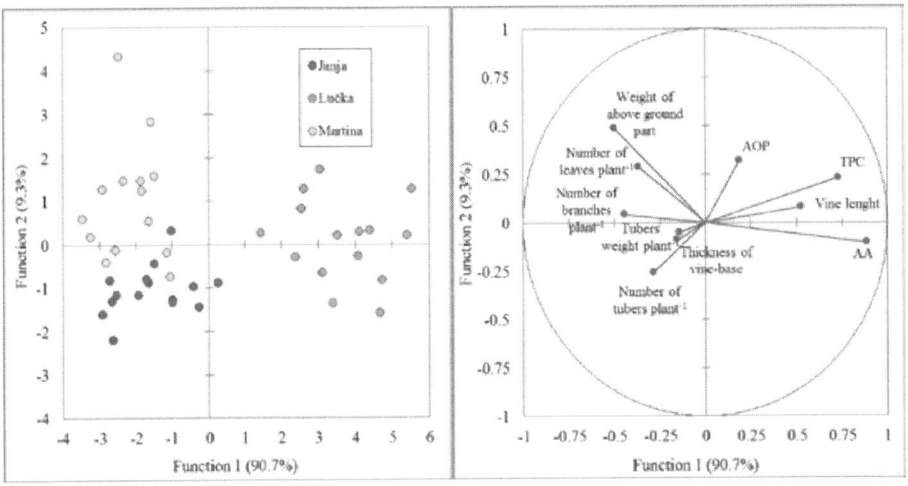

Figure 4. Discriminant analysis plot of observations (left) and variables chart (right) performed with the 10 traits: vine length, thickness of vine-base, number of branches, weight of above ground part, number of leaves plant^{-1}, number of tubers plant^{-1}, tubers weight plant^{-1}, TPC, AOP and AA; of the 15 samples originated from 3 sweetpotato cultivars ('Janja', 'Lučka' and 'Martina').

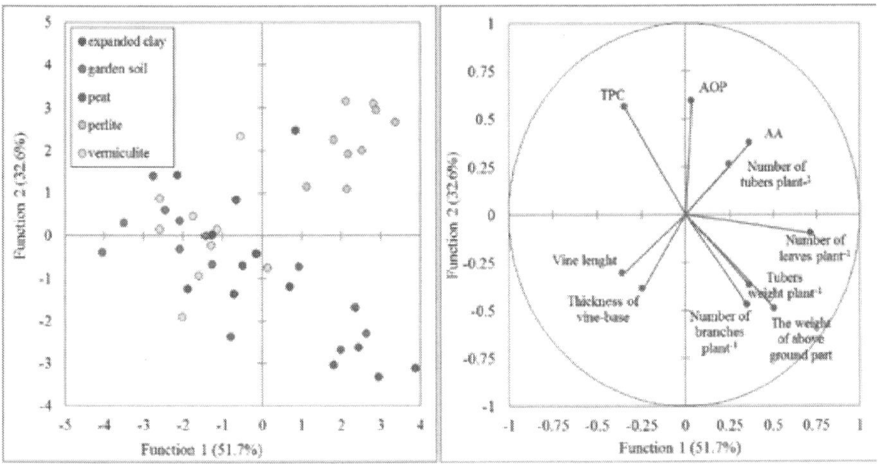

Figure 5. Discriminant analysis of observations (left) and variables chart (right) performed with the 10 traits: given in the legend of **Figure 4** (see also text); of the 15 sweetpotato samples cultivated in 5 different growing substrate (expanded clay, garden soil, peat, perlite and vermiculite).

vars 'Janja', 'Lučka' and 'Martina' were well separated, with the slight overlapping of groups 'Janja' and 'Martina' (one sample of 'Janja' and one of 'Martina' were in the opposite group).

Figure 5 shows the discrimination across the original data set of 15 samples cultivated in 5 different growing substrates (expanded clay, garden soil, peat, perlite and vermiculite). Discriminant analysis was carried out with the same 10 traits as given above. Function 1 explains 51.7% of the total variance and function 2 32.6% of the total variance. Major contributors to discriminate in function 1 between different growing substrate are AA, TPC, weight of above ground part and vine length, respectively; meanwhile the number of tubers plant^{-1}, TPC, AOP and vine length are major contributors in function 2. As seen from **Figure 5**, the sweetpotato samples grown in garden soil, vermiculite and expanded clay are located close to each other and on the other side of the score plot as those grown in perlite or peat. Sweetpotato samples grown in perlite and peat are clearly distinguished from the other growing substrate with slightly overlapping groups of peat and expanded clay (one sample of peat and one of expanded clay are in the opposite group).

4. Conclusions

The present study investigated the genetic differentiation among three new Slovenian sweetpotato cultivars ('Lučka', 'Janja' and 'Martina'). Results showed that the most genetically diverse variety is 'Martina'. Meanwhile, variety 'Lučka' possess the highest number of alleles which are unique and specific for this variety only. Global genetic variance among all three cultivars is 36%. The effect of different growing substrate (perlite, peat, expanded clay, vermiculite and garden soil) was examined for 10 agronomic and nutritional traits of these sweetpotato cultivars. Overall results show different response of cultivars in different growing substrate. Significant interactions of growing substrate × cultivar were observed for thickness of vine-base, weight of above ground part, AOP, TPC and AA. In conclusion, the discriminant analysis showed that the major traits for distinguishing among sweetpotato cultivars in function 1 are the AA, number of tubers plant^{-1}, tubers weight plant^{-1} and vine length, and in function 2 the weight of above ground part, TPC, AOP and number of tubers plant^{-1}; and between growing substrate in function 1 AA, TPC, weight of above ground part and vine length, and in function 2 the number of tubers plant^{-1}, TPC, AOP and vine length.

Acknowledgements

This book chapter has been prepared within the framework of the programs Horticulture (P4-0013) and Agrobiodiversity (P4-0072) funded by the Slovenian Research Agency.

References

[1] Austin DF, Huaman Z. A synopsis of Ipomoea (Convolvulaceae) in the Americas. Taxon. 1996;**45**:3-38

[2] Janick J. The great sweet/potato controversy. Horticulture. 1978;**42**:42-47

[3] Shekhar S, Mishra D, Buragohain AK, Chakraborty S, Chakraborty N. Comparative analysis of phytochemicals and nutrient availability in two contrasting cultivars of sweet potato (*Ipomoea batatas* L.). Food Chemistry. 2005;**173**:957-965

[4] Chandrasekara A, Joshephkumar T. Roots and tuber crops as functional foods: A review on phytochemical constituents and their potential health benefits. International Journal of Food Science. 2016;**2016**:1-15

[5] FAOSTAT. Food and agricultural statistical database. 2017. Available from: http://faostat.fao.org. [Accessed: 16-2-2017]

[6] Kunstelj N, Žnidarčič D, Šter B. Employing artificial neural networks and regression in analysis on knowledge about sweet potato (*Ipomoea batatas* L.) in Slovenia. Italian Journal of Food Science. 2013;**25**:263-274

[7] Kunstelj N, Žnidarčič D, Šter B. Using association rules mining for sweet potato (*Ipomoea batatas* L.) in Slovenia: A case study. Journal of Food Agriculture & Environment. 2015; **11**:253-258

[8] National list of Varieties. Republic of Slovenia, Ministry of Agriculture, Forestry and Food, The administration of the Republic of Slovenia for Food Safety, Veterinary Sector and Plant Protection. 2016. Available from: http://www.uvhvvr.gov.si/ [Accessed: 16-2-2017]

[9] Yamakawa O, Yoshimoto M. Sweetpotato as food material with physiological functions. Acta Horticulturae. 2002;**583**:179-184

[10] Teow CC, Truong VD, McFeeters RF, Thompson RL, Pecota KV, Yencho GC. Antioxidant activities, phenolic and β-carotene contents of sweet potato genotypes with varying flesh colours. Food Chemistry. 2007;**103**:829-838

[11] Tang Y, Cai W, Xu B. Profiles of phenolics, carotenoids and antioxidative capacities of thermal processed white, yellow, orange and purple sweet potatoes grown in Guilin, China. Food Science and Human Wellness. 2015;**4**:123-132

[12] Lebot V, Michalet S, Legendre L. Identification and quantification of phenolic compounds responsible for the antioxidant activity of sweet potatoes with different flesh colours using high performance thin layer chromatography (HPTLC). Journal of Food Composition and Analysis. 2016;**49**:94-101

[13] Ray RC, Panda SK, Swain MR, Sivakumar PS. Proximate composition and sensory evaluation of anthocyanin-rich purple sweet potato (*Ipomoea batatas* L.) wine. International Journal of Food Science & Technology. 2012;**47**:452-458

[14] Jung JK, Lee SU, Kozukue N, Levin CE, Friedman M. Distribution of phenolic compounds and antioxidative activities in parts of sweet potato (*Ipomoea batata* L.) plants and in home processed roots. Journal of Food Composition and Analysis. 2011;**24**:29-37

[15] Bovell-Benjamin AC. Sweet potato: A review of its past, present, and future role in human nutrition. Advances in Food and Nutrition Research. 2007;**52**:1-59

[16] Rumbaoa RGO, Cornago DF, Geronimo IM. Phenolic content and antioxidant capacity of Philippine sweet potato (*Ipomoea batatas*) varieties. Food Chemistry. 2009;**113**:1133-1138

[17] Oki T, Masuda M, Furuta S, Nishiba Y, Terahara N, Suda I. Involvement of anthocyanins and other phenolic compounds in radical-scavenging activity of purple-fleshed sweet potato cultivars. Journal of Food Science. 2002;**67**:1752-1756

[18] Padda MS, Picha DH. Quantification of phenolic acids and antioxidant activity in sweet-potato genotypes. Scientia Horticulturae. 2008;**119**:17-20

[19] Mukhtar AA, Tanimu B, Arunah UL, Babaji BA. Evaluation of the agronomic characters of sweet potato varieties grown at varying levels of organic and inorganic fertilizers. World Journal of Agricultural Sciences. 2010;**6**:370-373

[20] Kacjan Maršić N, Jakše M. Growth and yield of grafted cucumber (*Cucumis sativus* L.) on different soilless substrates. Journal of Food Agriculture & Environment. 2010;**8**:654-658

[21] Raviv M, Medina S. Physical characteristics of separated cattle manure compost. Compost Science & Utilization. 1997;**5**:44-47

[22] Grillas S, Lucas M, Bardopoulov E, Sarafopoulos S, Voulgari M. Perlite based soilless culture systems: Current commercial applications and prospects. Acta Horticulturae. 2001;**548**:105-113

[23] Gül A, Kidoğlu F, Anaç D. Effects of nutrient sources on cucumber production in different substrates. Scientia Horticulturae. 2007;**132**:216-220

[24] Szilágyi Z, Slezak K, Ferenczy A, Terbe I. Hydroponic pepper growing on baked clay pellets. International Journal of Horticultural Science. 2006;**12**:37-40

[25] Jankauskienė J, Brazaitytė A, Viškelis P. Effect of different growing substrates on physiological processes, productivity and quality of tomato in soilless culture. In: Asaduzzaman M, editor. Soilless Culture—Use of Substrates for the Production of Quality Horticultural Crops. Rijeka: InTech; 2015. pp. 99-124

[26] Rouin N, Caron J, Parent LE. Influence of some artificial substrates on productivity and DRIS diagnosis of greenhouse tomatoes (*Lycopersicum esculentum* L. Mill., cv. Vedettos). Acta Horticulturae. 1988;**221**:45-52

[27] Bilderback TE, Warren SL, Owen JS, Albano JP. Healthy substrates need physicals. HortTechnology. 2005;**15**:747-751

[28] Mastouri F, Hassandokht MR, Padasht Dehkaei MN. The effect of application of agricultural waste compost on growing media and greenhouse lettuce yield. Acta Horticulturae. 2005;**697**:153-158

[29] Rusjan D, Pelengić R, Pipan B, Or E, Javornik B, Štajner N. Israeli germplasm: Phenotyping and genotyping of native grapevines (*Vitis vinifera* L.). Vitis. 2015;**54**:87-89

[30] Pipan B, Šuštar-Vozlič J, Meglič V. Cultivation, varietal structure and possibilities for cross-pollination of *Brassica napus* L. in Slovenia. Acta Agiculturea Slovenica. 2011; **97**:247-258

[31] Pipan B, Šuštar-Vozlič J, Meglič V. Genetic differentiation among sexually compatible relatives of *Brassica napus* L. Genetika. 2013;**45**:309-327

[32] Pipan B, Žnidarčič D, Meglič V. Evaluation of genetic diversity of sweet potato [*Ipomoea batatas* (L.) Lam.] on different ploidy levels applying two capillary platforms. Journal of Horticultural Science and Biotechnology. 2016;**92**:192-198

[33] Maras M, Pipan B, Šuštar-Vozlič J, Todorović V, Đurić G, Vasić M, Kratovalieva S, Ibusoska A, Agić R, Matotan Z, Čupić T, Meglič V. Examination of genetic diversity of common bean from the Western Balkans. Journal of the American Society for Horticultural Science. 2015;**140**:208-316

[34] Derlink M, Pipan B, Pavlovčič P, Jones LE, Meglič V, Symondson WOC, Virant-Doberlet M. Characterization of eleven polymorphic microsatellite markers for leafhoppers of the genus Aphrodes (Hemiptera: Cicadellidae). Conservation Genetics Resources. 2014;**6**:933-935

[35] Veasey EA, Borges A, Silva Rosa M, Queiroz-Sila JR, de Andrade Bressan E, Peroni N. Genetic diversity in Brazilian sweet potato (*Ipomoea batats* (L.) Lam., Solanaes, Convolvulaceae) landraces assessed with microsatellite markers. Genetics and Molecular Biology. 2008;**31**:725-733

[36] Buteler MI, Jarret RL, DR LB. Sequence characterization of microsatellites in diploid and polyploid Ipomea. Theoretical and Applied Genetics. 1999;**99**:123-132

[37] Schuelke M. An economic method for the fluorescent labeling of PCR fragments. Nature Biotechnology. 2000;**18**:233-234

[38] Peakall R, Smouse PE. GENALEX 6: Genetic analysis in excel. population genetic software for teaching and research. Molecular Ecology Notes. 2006;**6**:288-295

[39] Roura E, Andrés-Lacueva C, Estruch R, Lamuela-Raventós RM. Total polyphenol intake estimated by a modified Folin-Ciocalteu assay of urine. Clinical Chemistry. 2006; **52**:749-752

[40] Nakajima JI, Tanaka I, Seo S, Yamazaki M, Saito K. LC/PDA/ESI-MS profiling and radical scavenging activity of anthocyanins in various berries. Journal of Biomedicine and Biotechnology. 2004;**5**:241-247

[41] Pipan B, Žnidarčič D, Kunstelj N, Meglič V. Genetic evaluation of sweet potato accessions introduced to the central European area. Journal of Agriculture Science and Technology. 2017;**19**:1139-1150

[42] Suárez MH, Hernández AIM, Galdón BR, Rodríguez LH, Cabrera CEM, Mesa DR, Rodríguez-Rodríguez EM, Romero CD. Application of multidimensional scaling technique to differentiate sweet potato (*Ipomoea batatas* (L.) Lam) cultivars according to their chemical composition. Journal of Food Composition and Analysis. 2016;**46**:43-49

Chapter 6

Sea Vegetables

Abstract

Sea vegetables or seaweeds have a long tradition in Asian cuisine. In Western countries, including Turkey, seaweed consumption is generally limited to sushi and other imported Asian dishes. However, seaweeds are well recognized for their richness in several nutrients such as carbohydrate, fiber, protein, lipid, and minerals. The migration of Asian population across the world has promoted the discovery of new ingredients from seaweeds and has given courage to the creation of new dishes by chefs in restaurants. Among the seaweeds traditionally consumed by Asian population, *Ulva, Laminaria,* and *Porphyra* are well-known species. Seaweed polysaccharides, such as agar, alginate, and carrageenan, are widely used in the food industry as clarifying, gelling, emulsifying, stabilizing, thickening, and flocculating agents in various food products such as ice cream, yogurt, candy, meat product, beverages, etc. The production of plant protein concentrates (PCs) is of growing interest to the food industry. Recently, PCs were also extracted from three edible green seaweed species of *Enteromorpha* or *Ulva*. Seaweed contains a wide array of nutritional compounds also possessing several functional properties that may lead to many dish and food preparation innovations. For example, a green seaweed, *Ulva,* may be used with or in the replacement of other commonly used vegetables to promote healthy food.

Keywords: algae, polysaccharide, proteins, fiber composition, minerals

1. Introduction

Algae, including micro-algae and macro-algae or seaweeds, constitute the primary producers in the aquatic food chain. Algae sustain the production of a hundred million tons per year of marine fisheries and a large portion of the aquaculture production, securing a stable human food supply. The annual seaweed production both from nature and aquaculture farms was 28.4 million tons in 2014, and 96% of seaweeds is produced by aquaculture with the value of 6.4 billion US dollar in 2013 [23]. About 40% of the seaweed production in 2014 represents seaweeds traditionally eaten in Japan. In 2014, 7.7 million of tons of Kombu (*Saccharina japonica*), 2.4 million tons of Wakame (*Undaria pinnatifida*), and 1.8 million tons of Nori (*Porphyra* sp.) which is particularly used dried in sushi preparation were produced [23]. Among the seaweeds, 13% have been used for the production of hydrocolloids (polysaccharides), such as agar, alginate or alginic acid, and carrageenan, while 75% are used for food, and the remaining (12%) are used by agriculture industry [34].

There has been a long traditional use of algae, especially seaweeds or sea vegetables, as food in Pacific and Asian countries for several centuries. In Pacific countries such as Indonesia, the Philippines, Maori of New Zealand, and Hawaii and Asian countries such as China, Japan, and Korea, seaweeds have long been consumed in a variety of dishes such as raw salads, soups, cookies, meals, and condiments [56]. In Iceland, Wales, France, as well as the Canadian and US Maritimes, there exists a traditional consumption of seaweed-based foods which varies in importance depending between country and regions but which is overall less prominent than in Asia [12].

The increase of vegetable consumption, including seaweeds, has been promoted to exert health benefits during Inuit childhood and life course [32, 43]. Thus, it is possible to see many cooking books incorporating recipes using "sea vegetables" in many countries around the world. And, more recently there has been a strong movement in European countries to introduce sea plants into the European cuisine. With the current trend for consumers, as "natural" food sources, marine plants receive an increasing acceptance [56].

All these advantages, together with available modern technologies and the proximity of European and Asian markets, encourage the development of sustainable seaweed cultivation for a variety of profitable end-products, such as protein, vitamins, minerals, phycocolloids, pigments, etc. In Turkey, algae cultivation is limited to micro-algae production in fish hatcheries. However, natural resources necessary for commercial seaweed cultivation, such as diversity of seaweed species, clean water, sunlight, and coastlines, are abundant. For example, in Turkey, more than 1000 seaweed species have been identified and species of *Porphyra, Gracilaria,* juvenile *Laminaria, Cystoseira, Sargassum,* and *Ulva* being particularly abundant [14]. In the overall Turkish population, the consumption of algae as a food is mostly limited to traditional algal cuisine from Asia [45, 84].

Seaweeds are well known for their abundance in several nutrients as dietary fibers, minerals (i.e., iodine), and certain vitamins (i.e., B12) and also contain numerous proteins/peptides, polyphenols, and polyunsaturated fatty acids (omega-3) [10]. A diet rich in seaweed in Asian countries has been consistently associated with a low incidence of cancers [13], and other potential health benefits of seaweeds have been reported, including cardioprotective, neuroprotective, and anti-inflammatory effects as well as beneficial impacts on gut function and microbiota [13]. These results not only strongly support the use of seaweeds in functional food development but also promote new utilization in food products and in the kitchen of consumers.

The objective of this chapter is to review the main uses of whole seaweeds in food formulations, including *Ulva,* and the interest of using some components such as seaweed polysaccharides and PCs as ingredients that could play roles in food as well as some nutritional attributes of seaweeds.

2. Seaweed utilization in food formulation

The recent popularity of sushi and Asian cuisine in Western countries, including Turkey, has stimulated the seaweed economy. The migration of Asian population across the world has promoted the discovery of new ingredients from seaweeds and has given courage to the creation of new dishes by chefs in restaurants. Among the seaweeds traditionally consumed by Asian population, *Ulva, Laminaria,* and *Porphyra* [1] are well-known species in addition to the other species used in Asian cuisine (**Table 1**). Species such as Wakame or Kombu requires cooking to overcome their chewy texture, while others can be eaten raw such as Nori and sea lettuce [59]. The valorization of seaweed as sea vegetables generally involves drying or salting processing treatments. Seaweed drying is one of the primary steps to allow their storage and transportation. They are either sun dried, air-dried, or dehydrated by salt addition [29, 87]. Seaweed can also be macerated with specific enzymes to improve protein bioaccessibility through hydrolysis of dietary fibers resistant to human digestion, but this process has not reached any commercial application yet [26, 29]. However, there are some recent studies on *Ulva lactuca* that is fermented with specific

Seaweed species	Common names
Alaria esculenta	Dabberlocks, Bladderlocks, Edible Kelp, Honeyware, Winged Kelp, Bladderlochs, Tangle, Henware, Murlins, Stringy Kelp, Horsetail kelp, Fruill, Rufaí, Láracha, Láir bhán, Sraoilleach, Láir, Essebarer Riementang, Marinkjarni, Chigaiso
Himanthalia elongata	Sea Spaghetti, Sea thong, Thongweed, Buttonweed, Sea Haricots, Thongweed
Hizikia fusiformis	Hijiki, Hai tso, Chiau tsai, Hai ti tun, Hai toe din, Hai tsao, Hoi tsou, Nongmichae
Laminaria digitata	Tangle, Sea girdles, Tangle tail, Wheelbangs, Sea wand, Sea ware, Sea Tangle, Horsetail Kelp, Kelp, Strap wrack, Oarweed, Oar weed, Horsetail tangle, Sea Girdle, Coirrleach, Screadhbhuidhe, Coirleach, Ribíní, Feamnach dhubh, Leathrach
Laminaria japonica or with its new name *Saccharina japonica*	Kombu, Hai Dai, Hai Tai, Kunpu, Royal Kombu, Makombu, Shinori-Kombu, Hababiro-Kombu, Oki-Kombu, Uchi Kombu, Moto-Kombu, Minmaya-Kombu, Ebisume, Hirome, Umiyama-Kombu, Hoiro-kombu, ae tae, Tasima
Undaria pinnatifida	Wakame, Qun dai cai, Sea mustard, Precious sea grass, Miyok, Miyeouk
Ulva lactuca	Sea lettuce, Tahalib, Hai Tsai, Shih shun, Haisai Kun-po, Kwanpo, Lettuce laver, Green Laver, Sea Grass, Thin stone brick, Chicory sea lettuce, Meersalat, Aosa, Klop-tsai-yup, Alface-do-mar, Luche, Luchi, Havssallat
Chondrus crispus	Irish Moss, Iers mos, Carragheen, Carragheen Moss, Dorset weed, Pearl Moss, Sea Moss, Sea Pearl Moss, Jelly Moss, Rock Moss, Gristle Moss, Curly Moss, Curly Gristle Moss, Carrageen, Carraghean, Carrageenin, Punalevä-laji, Cruibín chait, Carraigín, Cosáinín carriage, Irischmoos, Irisches moos, Muschio Irlandese, Musgo-gordo, Botelho, Botelha, Cuspelho, Musgo, Limo-folha, Musgo gordo, Folha-de-alface, Condrus, Karragener
Palmaria palmata	Dulse, Dillisk, Dillesk, Crannogh, Water Leaf, Sheep Dulse, Dried dulse, Shelldulse, Duileasc, Creathnach, Saccha, Sol, Darusu, Sou Sol, Botelho-comprido, Sea grass, American dulse, Dillisc, Sheep's weed, Sea devil, Horse seaweed, Creannach
Porphyra umbilicalis, Porphyra yezoensis, Porphyra tenera	Nori, Laverbread, Purple laver, Sloak, Slook, Laver, Tough, Chishima-kuronori, Folhuda

Table 1. Seaweed traditionally consumed as sea vegetable [69].

enzymes to improve protein bioaccessibility resistant to fish digestion [78]. During fermentation the growth of lactic acid bacteria was dependent on the seaweed species, the presence of fermentable carbohydrates such as laminaran, and the heating treatment applied prior to the inoculation step [33]. All these processing treatments are likely to affect seaweed's nutrients but to our knowledge, there are a limited number of studies describing their impact. More research may provide useful information to promote their usage in innovative dish and food preparation.

A green seaweed sea lettuce or *Ulva* is used in Scotland, where it is added to soups or used in salads, and today in Japan, where it is used in making sushi also with a red seaweed Nori or *Porphyra*. In Turkey, in the formulation of innovative seaweed dishes and food preparation samples, traditional mezze recipes belong to some vegetables replaced with *Ulva* (freshly harvested with 22.42% protein, dry weight) [84]. The seaweed dishes were prepared according to traditional recipes of stuffed grape leaves, spinach with rice, lamb's lettuce salad, *Salicornia* mezze, spicy tartare meatballs, and fresh sardines in grape leaves [3].

2.1. Food formulations of *Ulva*

The preparation of stuffed *Ulva* spp. for six servings according to the stuffed grape leave recipe started with soaking 225 g rice in warm and salted water for 10 min, followed by draining and rinsing. To prepare the filling, two onions were finely chopped, and two cloves of garlic were softened in two tablespoons of olive oil and a little butter. Then, one not quite full tablespoon of sugar, two tablespoons of currants soaked in water, and two tablespoons of pine nuts were added and cooked for 2–3 min. Next, one-half teaspoon of ground allspice, one-half teaspoon of ground cinnamon, and one-half teaspoon of ground cloves, salt, and freshly ground black pepper were added, and the mixture was covered with just enough water and brought to a boil. It was simmered for 10–15 min at reduced heat until the water was almost absorbed. Then, it was mixed with herbs (bunch of fresh parsley, dill, and mint) with a fork; the pan was covered and left for 5 min. The rice still had a bite to it. *Ulva* spp. were placed on the bottom of a wide pan. The rest of the *Ulva* spp., 24–30 pieces replacing a similar number of vine leaves in the original recipe, was laid on a flat surface, and a spoonful of the rice mixture was placed in the middle of each *Ulva*. The near end of each *Ulva* was folded over the mixture, and the side was flapped to seal it in and rolled up. The stuffed *Ulva* rolls were arranged in the pan, tightly packed. The cooking liquid—including 150 mL water, two tablespoons of olive oil, and two tablespoons of lemon juice—was poured over the rolls. A plate was placed on top to prevent them from unraveling, and the pan was covered with a lid. The liquid part was brought to a boil; then, the heat was reduced and cooked gently for 1 h. Finally, the rolls were left to cool in the pan and served cold with wedges of lemon (**Picture 1A**).

The preparation of *Ulva* spp. with rice according to a spinach with rice recipe for four to six servings started with frying one chopped onion with three to four cloves of garlic and one tablespoon of olive oil. Then, one glass of rinsed rice was added into the pan with some salt and black pepper and cooked for 2–3 min. Five hundred grams chopped fresh *Ulva*, instead of 500 g finely chopped fresh spinach, was added into the rice mixture, covered with just enough water, and brought to a boil. It was simmered for 10–15 min at reduced heat until the water was almost absorbed. The pan was then covered and left for 5 min (**Picture 1B**).

Picture 1. (A) Stuffed *Ulva*, (B) *Ulva* with rice, (C) *Ulva* salad, (D) sea lettuce *Ulva* mezze, (E) spicy tartare meatballs with *Ulva* spp., and (F) fresh sardines in *Ulva*.

In the preparation of *Ulva* salad according to a lamb's lettuce salad recipe for four to six servings, 500 g chopped fresh *Ulva* was used instead of 500 g lamb's lettuce. The chopped *Ulva* spp. were placed in a salad bowl, tossed in a little olive oil and lemon juice, and seasoned with salt and freshly ground black pepper. Two to three tablespoons of soft hick yogurt were mixed with two cloves of crushed garlic and added to the bowl; the mix was tossed well and served (**Picture 1C**).

In the preparation of *Ulva* mezze according to a *Salicornia* mezze recipe for four to six servings, 500 g chopped fresh *Ulva* was replaced with 500 g of *Salicornia*. The chopped *Ulva* spp. were placed in a salad bowl, tossed in a little olive oil and lemon juice, and seasoned with salt and freshly ground black pepper. Two cloves of crushed garlic were also added to the bowl; the mix was tossed well and served (**Picture 1D**).

Spicy tartare meatballs were prepared with *Ulva* spp. instead of lettuce leaves for four to six servings. Two hundred twenty-five grams of boiled bulgur was squeezed and allowed to cool (about 30 min), then put in a bowl with 225 g minced lamb or beef meat, and kneaded well (slapping it against the side of the bowl until well mixed). Two finely chopped onions, six finely chopped cloves of garlic, and two tablespoons of concentrated tomato purée were then kneaded into the mixture, followed by one teaspoon of red pepper, one-half teaspoon of roasted red pepper, one-half teaspoon of ground chili pepper, one-half teaspoon of ground coriander, one-half teaspoon of ground cumin, one-half teaspoon of ground allspice, one-half teaspoon of ground cinnamon, one-half teaspoon of ground cloves, one-half teaspoon of ground fenugreek, a little chopped parsley, and salt. The mixture was kneaded thoroughly for 20–30 min. Small portions of the mixture were then shaped into balls, indented with a finger, and arranged on a bed of parsley (**Picture 1E**).

***Ulva* was replaced with grape leaves in a dish filled with fresh sardines.** For four to six servings, 20–30 fresh sardines were wrapped in 25–30 *Ulva* spp., leaving the sardine heads peeping out. They were packed tightly in the base of a wide saucepan. Two tablespoons of olive oil, juice of one lemon, two crushed cloves of garlic, salt, and freshly ground black pepper were mixed to taste and poured over the sardines. A plate was placed directly on top of the sardines, the pan was covered, and it was cooked gently for 5–8 min. The dish was served hot or left to cool and sprinkled with salt or lemon juice (**Picture 1F**).

As it was seen, seaweeds contribute in a food either if they are used as a whole or through the numerous ingredients that have been produced from various species. In Turkey, *Hypnea musciformis* also known as Crozier weeds is a red seaweed species containing carrageenan, a gelling and thickening agent. Under its purified form, carrageenan is used by the food industry. Again, *Gracilaria gracilis* or *Gracilaria verrucosa* is a red seaweed species containing agar, a gelling and thickening agent. Under its purified form, agar is used by the food industry. *Cystoseira* spp. and *Sargassum vulgare* are brown seaweeds containing alginate or alginic acid with other important agents as well used by food industry.

2.2. Seaweed polysaccharides

Purified polysaccharides, such as agar, alginate, and carrageenan, are widely used in the food industry as clarifying, gelling, emulsifying, stabilizing, thickening, and flocculating agents in various food products such as ice cream, yogurt, candy, meat product, beverages, etc. The main structure and the functionality of polysaccharides extracted from seaweeds are presented in **Table 2**.

Agar and carrageenans are both found within red algae. Agar is mostly extracted from *Gelidium* and *Gracilaria* [56], and their cell wall holds up to 30% [31] and 20% [73], respectively. Agar structure is made of alternating d-galactose and l-galactose units (**Table 2**) [48, 60, 79]. It also contains (3,6)-anhydrogalactose rings and small amounts of sulfate groups (<4.5%) [40, 60]. Agar forms stable gels upon cooling between 32 and 43°C and at concentrations varying from 0.5 to 2% over a wide range of pH (**Table 2**). The gels are odorless and tasteless since no cations are necessary to promote the gel formation, and they are stable at temperature up to 85°C. The gel strength is influenced by the polysaccharide concentration, the number of 3,6-anhydrogalactose rings, the molecular weight, and the rate of cooling [6, 88]. One of agar gel characteristics is its in-mouth juiciness caused by the gel syneresis during mastication [62]. Agar gels are currently part of many traditional Japanese foods. Yokan (agar jelly with red bean paste), Mitsumame (canned fruit salad with agar jelly), and Tokoroten (noodlelike agar gel) are some examples of the culinary applications of agar [62, 79]. Worldwide, agar is also used as an additive in numerous food products such as dairy, bakery, and canned meat/fish products. It is also found in soups, sauces, and beverages. Carrageenans are sulfated polysaccharides extracted from seaweed such as *Chondrus crispus*, *Kappaphycus alvarezii*, and *Eucheuma denticulatum* [5, 56]. The seaweed cell wall can contain up to 80% of polysaccharides. Carrageenan's structure depends on the number of sulfate groups and (3,6)-anhydro-d-galactose rings (**Table 2**). The structure of carrageenans controls its gelling properties, and this has an important impact for its utilization in food systems. For example, the absence of (3,6)-anhydro-d-galactose ring units prevents λ-carrageenan gelation.

Polysaccharide	Main structure	Mw (kDa)	Solubility	Gelling condition and properties	Functional properties
Food grade polysaccharides					
Agar	(1,3)-α-d-galactose, (1,4)-β-l-galactose, 3,6-anhydrogalactose ring, <4.5% sulfate groups	36–386	>85°C	0.5–2%; melting 85°C	Clarifying, gelling, stabilizing, and flocculating agent
Alginate or alginic acid	β-d-mannuronic acid (M), α-l-guluronic acid (G) linked in β-(1,4) or α-(1,4)	150–1700	Salt, ionic strength, and pH	0.5–2%; melting 85°C; Ca or Mg	Gelling, emulsifying, film-forming, stabilizing, and thickening agent
Carrageenan	(1,3)-α-d-galactose, (1,4)-β-l-galactose, 3,6-anhydrogalactose ring, 25–35% sulfate groups	300–600	ι- > 70°C κ- > 70°C λ- cold	0.5–3%; ι- Ca melting 50–80°C; κ- Ca or K melting 40–75°C; λ- n/a	Gelling, thickening, suspension, and stabilizing agent
Mannitol	D-Mannitol monomers	n/a	nd	n/a	Sweetener, low glycemic index
Nonfood grade polysaccharides					
Fucoidan	α-(1,3) and α-(1,4)-l-fucose, <22% sulfate groups	6.8–1600	nd	None	None
Ulvan	β-d-glucuronosyluronic acid-(1,4)-α-l-rhamnose 3-sulfate, α-l-iduronopyranosic acid-(1,4)-α-l-rhamnose 3-sulfate, 15–20% sulfate groups	150–2000	nd	1.6%; Cu^{2+} and B^{3-}	None but potential gelling application

Mw, molecular weight; n/a, not applicable; nd, not determined.

Table 2. Seaweed polysaccharide structure and functionality [69].

Carrageenan may be found under three main structures influencing its gelling capacity. Lambda-carrageenan does not form gels but increases the solution viscosity to stabilize the overrun (whipped cream and shakes) or improve mouthfeel (pasteurized chocolate milk) [41]. It is also sometimes used in combination with κ-carrageenan to favor the formation of creamy gels (i.e., puddings and cream desserts) [39]. Kappa- and ι-carrageenans form gels at concentration varying between 0.5 and 3% and upon cooling at temperature ranging from 40 to 60°C in the presence of cations such as Ca or K [89]. Gels are thermally reversible at temperature up to 75 and 80°C for, respectively, κ- and ι-carrageenans and are stable at room temperature [39]. They are not only used in several water-based gelled desserts and cake frosting but also used in dairy products alone (flan, process cheese, sterilized chocolate, and evaporated milks) or in combination with other gums such as locust bean gum (cream cheese and ice cream). In brown seaweed, alginate may be isolated and found at concentrations up to 40% according to the seaweed species [57, 89].

Alginate is extracted from several brown algae including *Ascophyllum nodosum, Laminaria digitata, Laminaria hyperborea, Laminaria saccharina, Laminaria japonica, Ecklonia maxima, Macrocystis pyrifera, Lessonia nigrescens*, and *Lessonia trabeculata* [37, 56]. Alginate is a derivative of alginic acid, and it is found under the form of sodium, calcium, or magnesium alginate. It is composed of a mixture of β-d-mannuronic acid (M) and α-l-guluronic acid (G). These monomers are organized in segments containing MM, GG, or MG/GM blocks which are linked β-(1,4) for MG block or α-(1,4) in the case of GG block. The proportion of each segment affects the gelling properties of alginate. Alginate containing high amounts of GG blocks will lead to firm and rigid gel [20]. Alginate is used as a thickening agent in ice cream, ketchup, mayonnaise, sauces, and purees [57, 89]. The viscosity of the solution may be controlled by the addition of Ca. Alginate gelling property is useful in several food applications such as jams, puddings, and restructured food (chili found in green olives or onion rings made with onion powder). Its film-forming capacity reduces water loss and regulates water diffusion in food products [37]. The pastries fruit filling is often covered with an alginate film to prevent cake moistening.

The food industry in collaboration with polysaccharide suppliers has developed a thorough knowledge regarding the usage of algal polysaccharides in food products. However, the culinary usages might at some point be less known by chefs. Recently, the culinary use of those purified ingredients was reviewed in the book *Modernist Cuisine* [61]. The functional properties such as solubility, foaming, as well as gelation are potentialized and presented for culinary purposes. For example, agar gels may be used in terrine (appetizer), agar beads flavored with fruit or vegetable juices, Chantilly without cream, pasta, eggless mayonnaise, foams, etc. Alginate main usages in modern cuisine are under the form of moldable forms (spaghetti, beads, etc.). Propylene glycol alginate may also be used to produce eggless citrus curd [61]. The proper combination of κ - and ι-carrageenans allowed the formation of a dashi-flavored gel to coat cremini mushrooms [61]. Also, these polysaccharides may be used in combination to stabilize a beurre blanc sauce emulsion, processed cheese, etc.

Finally, other polysaccharides such as fucoidan and ulvan could potentially be interesting for culinary applications. Fucoidan is a sulfated polysaccharide mainly of l-fucose (>50%), and up to 10% of this polysaccharide was isolated in several brown seaweeds [42, 83]. Fucoidan is not used as a food ingredient in Turkey but is included in food as a nutraceutical in Asia [25]. This polysaccharide has no gelling or thickening capacity (Rioux et al., 2007) as compared to others such as alginate. However, when the whole brown seaweed Kombu or Wakame is consumed, substantial amount of fucoidan may be ingested and have beneficial effects in humans. Ulvan is a water-soluble polysaccharide found within green algae *Ulva* spp. The algae contains between 8 and 29% ulvan on dry basis [47]. Ulvan is mainly composed in l-rhamnose and d-glucuronic acid under the form of ulvanobiuronic acids A and B [46, 67]. Ulvan molecular weight ranges between 150 and 2000 kDa depending on the extraction method and seaweed species [64, 77, 91]. Ulvan possesses interesting gelling and viscosifying properties dictated by the amount of uronic acids that may be useful in food products [76, 77, 90]. Most recent studies were oriented toward biomedical applications [58, 86]. This polysaccharide could be of interest for new food application.

2.3. Seaweed protein concentrates (PCs)

The production of plant protein concentrates (PCs) is of growing interest to the food industry [81]. Recently, PCs were extracted from three edible green seaweed species of *Enteromorpha* or *Ulva* and were investigated for their functional properties as functions of salt and pH [44]. The protein contents in the PCs varied from around 33 to 60%. In all three PCs, the minimum nitrogen solubility was observed at pH 4, and foaming capacity and stability were pH-specific. Also, PC of red alga *Kappaphycus* was extracted, and its functional properties were evaluated [81]. The PC contained around 62% proteins, and the results obtained in this investigation suggest great emulsion stability with oil extracted from Jatropha, a plant species of the Euphorbiaceae family native to Brazil. Although these results are promising, before considering these PCs as ingredients in food formulations, food-grade solvents have to be chosen during the extraction method avoiding chemical residues, which could be toxic [69]. Indeed, solvent choice influences potential applications of algal protein extracts in terms of human consumption [75].

3. Nutritional contribution of seaweeds

Seaweed's main constituents vary according to the seaweed species, harvest location and time, wave exposition, and water temperature. Also, the methodology used to determine these constituents may differ which may explain why large variations are sometimes observed (**Table 3**). Seaweeds are rich in carbohydrates, and concentration up to 76% of the algae dry weight was reported. Also, an important proportion of proteins was quantified. *Ulva* sp. contains up to 44% of proteins based on the algae dry weight. The mineral content also reaches values as high as 55% that were found for *Ulva* sp. Generally, seaweed lipid content is relatively low (<5%) independently of the species.

3.1. Seaweed carbohydrates

Seaweed carbohydrates or polysaccharides are mostly found within the algae cell wall with exception of the storage polysaccharides which are located in the plastid. The seaweed cell wall (extracellular matrix) has an important structural role. It is a physical barrier against wave, ice,

Seaweed species	Polysaccharide (%)	Protein (%)	Lipid (%)	Ash (%)
Ulva sp.	15–65	4–44	0.3–1.6	26; 52–55
Laminaria longicruris or *Saccharina longicruris*	38–61	3–21	0.3–2.9	15–45
Ascophyllum nodosum and *Fucus vesiculosus*	42–70	1.2–17	0.5–4.8	18–30
Undaria pinnatifida	35 15	11 21	1 1.5	27 10; 11
Sargassum sp.	68	9–20	0.5–3.9	44
Chondrus crispus	55–66	6–29	0.7–3	21
Porphyra sp.	40–76	7–50	0.12–2.8	7–21
Gracilaria sp.	36; 62–63	5–23	0.4–2.6	8–29
Palmaria palmata	38–74	8–35	0.2–3.8	12-37

Values are expressed in percentage (%) of dry weight.

Table 3. Composition of different seaweed species [69].

and sun dehydration [65], but it also regulates many other functions such as solute accumulation, turgor, and cell growth [8, 68]. The main cell wall polysaccharides are agar and carrageenan (Rhodophyta), sulfated fucans and alginates (Ochrophyta), and cellulose and hemicellulose (Chlorophyta). Seaweeds within the Ochrophyta and Rhodophyta phyla also contain variable amounts of cellulose and/or hemicellulose according to the seaweed species [2, 18].

The storage carbohydrates are equivalent to the human glycogen and serve as the principal energy source [9]. According to the seaweed species, other small polysaccharides may be found within the chloroplast (laminaran and starch) or in the cytoplasm (floridean starch) [85]. Smaller solutes are found when seaweeds are grown under high salinity conditions. Mannitol, sucrose, floridoside, isofloridoside, and digeneaside were reported for some seaweed. They can serve as photosynthetic reserve or as osmoregulator [19, 68].

3.1.1. Seaweed fiber composition

Seaweeds are good sources of fibers since they contain valuable carbohydrates undigested by the human gastrointestinal track [69]. Dietary fibers, or fibers from food source, remain intact in the small intestine while they are partially or sometimes completely fermented by the gut microbiota [24]. The total dietary fiber within food may be found under two forms, such as soluble and insoluble, depending on the polysaccharide structure. Soluble fibers refer to polysaccharides that may be solubilized in water. They are known to increase the viscosity in the gastrointestinal track and are fermented by the microbiota. At the opposite, insoluble fibers have a bulking action and are rarely fermented [69]. Seaweeds with their high polysaccharide contents (**Table 2**) have interesting nutritional properties since their total dietary fiber may reach up to 38% (dry weight) according to the seaweed species [29]. Among them, some polysaccharides are already considered as valuable food ingredients and are, therefore, available on the market as purified polysaccharides such as agar, alginate, and carrageenan.

3.2. Seaweed proteins

Increasing world population and the consumer demand for healthy foods have driven the search for unconventional protein sources as ingredients to be incorporated in new high-value products [15, 52, 70]. Seaweeds have long been used in Asia as traditional foodstuffs [22]. Also, they have been recently promoted in the cuisine of several American and European countries and evaluated for the nutritional value of their proteins, which is mainly defined by their amino acid composition and digestibility [56]. Proteins are present in algae in a variety of forms and distributed in various cellular compartments. They are part of the intracellular components or the cell wall, are enzymes, or are bound to pigments and polysaccharides [80]. The protein content is variable according to the species, season, geographic distribution, population, cultivation conditions, and nutrient supply during growth phase [4, 17, 27, 36, 52, 54]. In general, the red and green species contain relatively high protein levels, with an average value of 4–50% (w/w) dry weight, compared to brown species, which contain between 1 and 29% (w/w) dry weight (**Table 3**) [35]. The protein concentrations of red species are comparable to those found in high-protein vegetables such as soybeans where proteins represent 35% of the dry weight [63]. A review of the nutrient composition of edible seaweeds has been reported comparing different protein contents of red, green, and brown species [66].

Seaweed proteins display a very good profile of essential amino acids, which is equivalent to other food proteins such as legumes or eggs [28], and their levels are comparable to those of the FAO/WHO requirements of dietary proteins [63]. Algal proteins usually contain most amino acids particularly glycine, alanine, arginine, proline, and glutamine and aspartic acids [11]. Both aspartic and glutamic acids are abundant in most seaweed species (brown, red, and green), and they exhibit interesting features in flavor development. Hence, glutamic acid is the main component in the taste sensations of umami [63], and the average proportion is higher in brown seaweed (153 mg/g proteins) compared to the red (117 mg/g proteins) and green (119 mg/g proteins) seaweeds [21]. In comparison with other protein-rich food sources, seaweeds are limited by lysine, threonine, tryptophan, and sulfur amino acids (cysteine and methionine), even though their levels are generally higher than those found in vegetables and cereals [38]. Seaweeds contain a proportion of free amino acids including taurine, alanine, amino butyric acid, ornithine, citrulline, and hydroxyproline. Numerous seaweed species also contain unusual amino acids among those, mycosporine-like amino acids (MAAs) known as demonstrating antioxidant properties [35].

3.3. Seaweed lipids

Seaweeds contain relatively low levels of lipids (1–5%) when compared to other plant seeds such as soy and sunflower, but majority of those lipids are polyunsaturated fatty acids (PUFAs) [50, 51]. PUFA's health benefits are well documented for fish, and seaweeds may also provide a sustainable source of these compounds. Algal PUFAs are under the form of ω-3 fatty acids such as eicosapentaenoic acid (EPA, C20:5) or docosahexaenoic acid (DHA, C22:6). EPA and DHA may both be metabolized from α-linolenic acid (ALA, C18:3), an essential fatty acid not only synthesized by humans but also found in seaweeds. Red seaweeds can contain up to 50% of EPA, while much lower levels were found in brown species [30]. Amounts of ω-6 fatty acids such as arachidonic acid (ARA, C20:4) are also found in seaweeds, and their levels are equivalent to the proportion of ω-3 with an ω-6/ω-3 ratio that is ranging from 0.1 to 1.5 [16, 50]. This is particularly interesting since a balanced ω-6/ω-3 ratio was associated to a decreased risk of mortality. Readers are referred to recent review papers discussing the health benefits of algal PUFAs for more details [7, 10].

The lipid content and fatty acid composition of seaweeds vary by species, geographical location, season temperature, salinity, and light intensity [72]. Based on the fatty acid composition and potential health benefits such as anti-inflammatory activity, seaweed species could be selected for cultivation toward food and health markets [55]. The lipid characterization of cultivated seaweeds during a year-round could contribute to a better control in aquaculture settings in order to identify the best harvest time for the choice of lipid quantity and quality. For example, PUFAs are made up more than half of the fatty acids with a maximum in July for *Saccharina latissima* cultivated in Denmark [53]. In addition, the *Saccharina latissima* species presents a better source of PUFAs compared to traditional vegetables, such as cabbage and lettuce.

The growing interest in PUFA-rich lipids from seaweeds for incorporation into foods has led to look for alternative extraction techniques with higher yields together with food grade solvent uses. As a result, the highest levels of PUFAs were obtained by the extraction with ethanol [74]. Seaweeds are also generally tested after food processing (drying, canning, etc.), due to its possible detrimental effect on fatty acid levels [72].

3.4. Seaweed minerals

The mineral content of seaweed is of great importance since up to 45% of the algal dry mass may be found (**Table 3**) [71, 82]. The values varied according to the seaweed species, seasonal variation, harvest time, and location [49]. Seaweed contains several mineral elements required in human nutrition such as Na, K, Ca, Mg, Fe, Zn, Mn, and Cu. For example, 948 and 2782 mg/100 dry weight of Ca were found, respectively, for *Gracilaria salicornia* and *Ulva lactuca*. These values are much higher than the one found in terrestrial plants such as spinach (851 mg/100 dry weight), broccoli (503 mg/100 dry weight), and cabbage (369 mg/100 dry weight) [82]. Their elevated amount in I content is one important feature of seaweeds. Holdt and Kraan [38] have reviewed that the distribution within several seaweed species including *Laminaria* sp. contains up to 8000 times of the recommended daily value.

4. Conclusions

Seaweed contains a wide array of nutritional compounds also possessing several functional properties that may lead to many dish and food preparation innovations. For example, seaweeds may be used with or in the replacement of other commonly used vegetables to promote healthy food. Until now only few applications have been taking profit of both attributes, and this should be more deeply exploited in the future. Collaboration with creative chefs can increase the visibility and acceptance of this resource by offering recipes or dishes where seaweeds are displayed. Future work connecting culinary and food science may support the usage of seaweeds not only at home but also in food products.

References

[1] Atlas RM, Bartha R. Microbial Ecology: Fundamentals and Applications. 4th ed. Menlo Park, CA, USA: Benjamin/Cummings; 1998, 694 p

[2] Barsanti L, Gualtieri P. Algae: Anatomy, Biochemistry, and Biotechnology. 2nd ed. Boca Raton: CRC Press; 2014. 361 p

[3] Basan G. Classical Turkish Cooking. New York, NY: St. Martin's Press; 2000. 224 p

[4] Beaulieu L, Sirois M, Tamigneaux E. Evaluation of the in vitro biological activity of protein hydrolysates of the edible red alga, Palmaria palmata (dulse) harvested from the Gaspe coast and cultivated in tanks. Journal of Applied Phycology. 2016;**28**:3101-3115

[5] Bixler HJ, Johndro KD. Philippine natural grade or semi-refined carrageenan. In: Phillips GO, Williams PA, editors. Handbook of Hydrocolloids. Boca Raton: CRC Press LLC; 2000. pp. 425-442

[6] Boral S, Saxena A, Bohidar HB. Universal growth of microdomains and gelation transition in agar hydrogels. The Journal of Physical Chemistry B. 2008;**112**(12):3625-3632

[7] Brown EM, Allsopp PJ, Magee PJ, Gill CIR, Nitecki S, Strain CR. Seaweed and human health. Nutrition Reviews. 2014;**72**:205-216

[8] Brownlee C. Role of the extracellular matrix in cell–cell signalling: Paracrine paradigms. Current Opinion in Plant Biology. 2002;**5**:396-401

[9] Busi MV, Barchiesi J, Martín M, Gomez-Casati DF. Starch metabolism in green algae. Starch/Staerke. 2014;**66**:28-40

[10] Cardoso SM, Pereira OR, OR SAM, Pinto DC, Silva A. Seaweeds as preventive agents for cardiovascular diseases: From nutrients to functional foods. Marine Drugs. 2015; **13**:6838-6865

[11] Cerna M. Seaweed proteins and amino acids as nutraceuticals. Advances in Food and Nutrition Research. 2011;**64**:297-312

[12] Chopin T. Marine aquaculture in Canada: Well-established monocultures of finfish and shellfish and an emerging integrated multi-trophic aquaculture (IMTA) approach including seaweeds, other invertebrates, and microbial communities. Fisheries. 2015;**40**:28-31

[13] Cian RE, Drago SR, de Medina FS, Martínez-Augustin O. Proteins and carbohydrates from red seaweeds: Evidence for beneficial effects on gut function and microbiota. Marine Drugs. 2015;**13**:5358-5383

[14] Cirik Ş, Cirik S. Aquatic plants: Biology, ecology and cultivations techniques of marine plants. Izmir, Turkey: Ege University, Fisheries Faculty Publications, no:28; 2017. 188 p. ISBN 975-483-46-4 (in Turkish)

[15] Cole AJ, de Nys R, Paul NA. Biorecovery of nutrient waste as protein in freshwater macroalgae. Algal Research. 2015;**7**:58-65

[16] Colombo ML, Risè P, Giavarini F, De Angelis L, Galli C, Bolis CL. Marine macroalgae as sources of polyunsaturated fatty acids. Plant Foods Human Nutrition. 2006;**61**(2):64-69

[17] Connan S, Deslandes E, Gall EA. Influence of day–night and tidal cycles on phenol content and antioxidant capacity in three temperate intertidal brown seaweeds. Journal of Experimental Marine Biology and Ecology. 2007;**349**:359-369

[18] Cronshaw J, Myers A, Preston RD. A chemical and physical investigation of the cell walls of some marine algae. Biochimica et Biophysica Acta. 1958;**27**:89-103

[19] Dittami SM, Gravot A, Renault D, Goulitquer S, Eggert A, Bouchereau A. Integrative analysis of metabolite and transcript abundance during the short-term response to saline and oxidative stress in the brown alga *Ectocarpus siliculosus*. Plant Cell & Environment. 2011;**34**:629-642

[20] Draget KI, SkjakBraek G, Smidsrod O. Alginate based new materials. International Journal of Biological Macromolecules. 1997;**21**:47-55

[21] Dumay J, Morançais M. Proteins and pigments. In: Fleurence J, Levine I, editors. Seaweed in Health and Disease Prevention. San Diego, CA, USA: Academic Press; 2016. pp. 275-318

[22] FAO. The State of World Fisheries and Aquaculture. Italy, Rome: FAO; 2014

[23] FAO. FAO Fishery and Aquaculture Statistics. Global Production by Production Source 1950-2014. FishstatJ; 2016. http://www.fao.org/fishery/statistics/software/fishstatj/en [Accessed: September 2, 2016]

[24] FAO/WHO. FAO/WHO Guidelines on Nutrition Labelling. Rome; 2013

[25] Fitton JH, Irhimeh MR, Teas J. Marine algae and polysaccharides with therapeutic applications. In: Barrow C, Shahidi F, editors. Marine Nutraceuticals and Functional Foods. Boca Raton, FL, USA: CRC Press; 2008. pp. 345-366

[26] Fleurence J. The enzymatic degradation of algal cell walls: A useful approach for improving protein accessibility? Journal of Applied Phycology. 1999;**11**:313-314

[27] Fleurence J. Seaweed proteins: Biochemical, nutritional aspects and potential uses. Trends in Food Science & Technology. 1999;**10**:25-28

[28] Fleurence J. Seaweed proteins. In: Yada R, editor. Proteins in Food Processing. Cambridge, UK: Woodhead Publishing Limited; 2004. pp. 197-213

[29] Fleurence J. Seaweeds as food. In: Fleurence J, Levine I, editors. Seaweed in Health and Disease Prevention. San Diego, CA, USA: Academic Press; 2016. pp. 149-167

[30] Fleurence J, Gutbier G, Mabeau S, Leray C. Fatty acids from 11 marine macroalgae of the French Brittany coast. Journal of Applied Phycology. 1994;**6**:527-532

[31] Freilepelegrin Y, Robledo DR, Garciareina G. Seasonal agar yield and quality in Gelidium canariensis (grunow) Seoane-camba (gelidiales, rhodophyta) from Gran canaria, Spain. Journal of Applied Phycology. 1995;**7**:141-144

[32] Gagné D, Blanchet R, Lauzière J, Vaissière E, Vézina C, Ayotte P. Traditional food consumption is associated with higher nutrient intakes in Inuit children attending childcare centres in Nunavik. International Journal of Circumpolar Health. 2012;**71**:1-9

[33] Gupta S, Abu-Ghannam N, Scannell AGM. Growth and kinetics of Lactobacillus plantarum in the fermentation of edible Irish brown seaweeds. Food and Bioproducts Processing. 2011;**89**:346-355

[34] Hardouin K, Bedoux G, Burlot AS, Nyvall-Collén P, Bourgougnon N. Enzymatic recovery of metabolites from seaweeds: Potential applications. In: Nathalie B, editor. Advances in Botanical Research, Vol. 71. Academic Press; 2014. pp. 279-320

[35] Harnedy PA, FitzGerald RJ, 2011. Bioactive proteins, peptides, and amino acids from macroalgae. Journal of Phycology, 47, 218-232

[36] Harnedy PA, Soler-Vila A, Edwards MD, FitzGerald RJ. The effect of time and origin of harvest on the in vitro biological activity of Palmaria palmata protein hydrolysates. Food Research International. 2014;**62**:746-752

[37] Helgerud T, Gåserød O, Fjæreide T, Andersen PO, Larsen CK. Alginates, Food Stabilisers, Thickeners and Gelling Agents. Ames, IA, USA: Wiley-Blackwell; 2009. pp. 50-72

[38] Holdt SL, Kraan S. Bioactive compounds in seaweed: Functional food applications and legislation. Journal of Applied Phycology. 2011;**23**:543-597

[39] Imeson AP. Carrageenan. In: Phillips GO, Williams PA, editors. Handbook of Hydrocolloids. Boca Raton, FL, USA: CRC Press LLC; 2000. pp. 87-102

[40] Imeson AP. Agar. In: Imeson A, editor. Food Stabilisers, Thickeners and Gelling Agents. Oxford, UK: Wiley-Blackwell; 2009. pp. 31-49

[41] Imeson AP. Carrageenan and furcellaran. In: Phillips GO, Williams PA, editors. Handbook of Hydrocolloids, 2nd ed. Cambridge, UK: Woodhead Publishing; 2009. pp. 164-185

[42] Indegaard M, Minsaas J. Animal and human nutrition. In: Guiry MD, Blunden G, editors. Seaweed Resources in Europe. Uses and Potential. Chichester, UK: John Wiley & Sons; 1991. pp. 21-64

[43] Johnson-Down L, Egeland GM. Adequate nutrient intakes are associated with traditional food consumption in Nunavut Inuit children aged 3-5 years. The Journal of Nutrition. 2010;**140**:1311-1316

[44] Kandasamy G, Karuppiah SK, Subba Rao PV. Salt- and pH-induced functional changes in protein concentrate of edible green seaweed Enteromorpha species. Fisheries Science. 2011;**78**:169-176

[45] Kilic B, Cirik S, Turan G, Tekogul H, Koru E. Seaweeds for food and industrial applications. In: Muzzalupo I, editor. Food Industry. Croatia: InTech; 2013. pp. 735-748, Chapter 31. DOI: 10.5772/55834

[46] Lahaye M, Ray B. Cell-wall polysaccharides from the marine green alga Ulva rigida Ulvales, Chlorophyta—NMR analysis of ulvan oligosaccharides. Carbohydrate Research. 1996;**283**:161-173

[47] Lahaye M, Robic A. Structure and function properties of Ulvan, a polysaccharide from green seaweeds. Biomacromolecules. 2007;**8**:1765-1774

[48] Lahaye M, Rochas C. Chemical structure and physico-chemical properties of agar. Hydrobiologia. 1991;**221**:137-148

[49] Mabeau S, Fleurence J. Seaweed in food products—Biochemical and nutritional aspects. Trends in Food Science & Technology. 1993;**4**:103-107

[50] MacArtain P, Gill CIR, Brooks M, Campbell R, Rowland IR. Nutritional value of edible seaweeds. Nutrition Reviews. 2007;**65**:535-543

[51] Makkar HP, Tran G, Heuzé V, Giger-Reverdin S, Lessire M, Lebas F. Seaweeds for livestock diets: A review. Animal Feed Science and Technology. 2016;**212**:1-17

[52] Marinho GS, Holdt SL, Angelidaki I. Seasonal variations in the amino acid profile and protein nutritional value of *Saccharina latissima* cultivated in a commercial IMTA system. Journal of Applied Phycology. 2015a;**27**:1991-2000

[53] Marinho GS, Holdt SL, Jacobsen C, Angelidaki I. Lipids and composition of fatty acids of *Saccharina latissima* cultivated year-round in integrated multi-trophic aquaculture. Marine Drugs. 2015;**13**:4357-4374

[54] Martínez B, Rico JM. Seasonal variation of p content and major n pools in Palmaria palmata (Rhodophyta). Journal of Phycology. 2002;**38**:1082-1089

[55] McCauley JI, Meyer BJ, Winberg PC, Ranson M, Skropeta D. Selecting Australian marine macroalgae based on the fatty acid composition and anti-inflammatory activity. Journal of Applied Phycology. 2015;**27**:2111-2121

[56] McHugh DJ. A Guide to the Seaweed Industry. Rome, Italy: FAO; 2003, 441 p

[57] Moe ST, Draget KI, Skjåk-Braek G, Smidsrød O. Alginates. In: Stephen AM, editor. Food Polysaccharides and Their Applications. New York: Marcel Dekker; 1995. pp. 245-286

[58] Morelli A, Betti M, Puppi D, Chiellini F. Design, preparation and characterization of ulvan based thermosensitive hydrogels. Carbohydrate Polymers. 2016;**136**:1108-1117

[59] Mouritsen OG. Sushi: Food for The Eye, The Body, & The Soul. New York, NY, USA: Springer Science; 2009. 330 p

[60] Murano E. Chemical structure and quality of agars from Gracilaria. Journal of Applied Phycology. 1995;**7**:245-254

[61] Myhrvold N, Young C, Bilet M. Modernist Cuisine: The Art and Science of Cooking—Ingredients and Preparations. Vol. 4. Bellevue, WA, USA: The Cooking Lab, LLC; 2011

[62] Nussinovitch A, Hirashima M. Agar-agar. In: Nussinovitch A, Hirashima M, editors. Cooking Innovations: Using Hydrocolloids for Thickening, Gelling, and Emulsification. Boca Raton, FL, USA: CRC Press; 2013. pp. 1-22

[63] Pangestuti R, Kim SK. Seaweed proteins, peptides, and amino acids. In: Tiwari BK, Troy DJ, editors. Seaweed Sustainability. San Diego, CA, USA: Academic Press; 2015. pp. 125-140

[64] Paradossi G, Cavalieri F, Chiessi E. A conformational study on the algal polysaccharide ulvan. Macromolecules. 2002;**35**:6404-6411

[65] Percival E. The polysaccharides of green, red and brown seaweeds: Their basic structure, biosynthesis and function. British Phycological Journal. 1979;**14**:103-117

[66] Pereira L. A review of the nutrient composition of selected edible seaweeds. In: Pomin VH, editor. Seaweed: Ecology, Nutrient Composition and Medicinal Uses. Hauppauge, NY, USA: Nova Science Publishers, Inc; 2011. pp. 15-47

[67] Quemener B, Lahaye M, Bobin-Dubigeon C. Sugar determination in ulvans by a chemical-enzymatic method coupled to high performance anion exchange chromatography. Journal of Applied Phycology. 1997;**9**:179-188

[68] Reed RH, 2010. Solute accumulation and osmotic adjustment. K.M. Cole, R.G. Sheath (Eds.), Biology of the Red Algae, Cambridge University Press, Cambridge, pp. 147-170

[69] Rioux LE, Beaulieui L, Turgeon S. Seaweeds: A traditional ingredients for new gastronomic sensation. Food Hydrocolloids. 2017;**68**:255-265

[70] Rosegrant MW, Cline SA. ClineGlobal food security: Challenges and policies. Science. 2003;**302**:1917-1919

[71] Ruperez P. Mineral content of edible marine seaweeds. Food Chemistry. 2002;**79**:23-26

[72] Sánchez-Machado D, López-Cervantes J, López-Hernández J, Paseiro-Losada P. Fatty acids, total lipid, protein and ash contents of processed edible seaweeds. Food Chemistry. 2004;**85**:439-444

[73] Santelices B, Doty MS. A review of Gracilaria farming. Aquaculture. 1989;**78**:95-133

[74] Schmid M, Guihéneuf F, Stengel DB. Evaluation of food grade solvents for lipid extraction and impact of storage temperature on fatty acid composition of edible seaweeds Laminaria digitata (Phaeophyceae) and Palmaria palmata (Rhodophyta). Food Chemistry. 2016;**208**:161-168

[75] Shannon E, Abu-Ghannam N. Antibacterial derivatives of marine algae: An overview of pharmacological mechanisms and applications. Marine Drugs. 2016;**14**(4):1-23

[76] Shao P, Qin M, Han L, Sun P. Rheology and characteristics of sulfated polysaccharides from chlorophytan seaweeds Ulva fasciata. Carbohydrate Polymers. 2014;**113**:365-372

[77] Siddhanta AK, Goswami AM, Ramavat BK, Mody KH, Mairh OP. Water soluble polysaccharides of marine algal species of Ulva (Ulvales, Chlorophyta) of Indian waters. Indian Journal of Marine Sciences. 2001;**30**:166-172

[78] Spigel M, Guttman L, Shauli L, Odintsov V, Ben-Ezra D, Harpaz S. Ulva lactuca from an integrated multi-trophic aquaculture (IMTA) biofilter system as a protein supplement in gilthead seabream (Sparus aurata) diet. Aquaculture. 2017;**434**:112-118

[79] Stanley NF. Agars. In: Stephen AM, Phillips GO, Williams PA, editors. Food Polysaccharides and Their Applications. 2nd ed. Boca Raton, FL, USA: Taylor & Francis Group; 2006. pp. 217-238

[80] Stengel DB, Connan S, Popper ZA. Algal chemodiversity and bioactivity: Sources of natural variability and implications for commercial application. Biotechnology Advances. 2011;**29**:483-501

[81] Suresh Kumar K, Ganesan K, Selvaraj K, Subba Rao PV. Studies on the functional properties of protein concentrate of Kappaphycus alvarezii (Doty) Doty–An edible seaweed. Food Chemistry. 2014;**153**:353-360

[82] Tabarsa M, Rezaei M, Ramezanpour Z, Waaland JR. Chemical compositions of the marine algae Gracilaria salicornia (Rhodophyta) and Ulva lactuca (Chlorophyta) as a potential food source. Journal of the Science of Food and Agriculture. 2012;**92**:2500-2506

[83] Turan G, Cirik S, Tekogul H, Koru E, Karacalar U, Seyhaneyıldız Can Ş. Determination of the seasonal yields of total fucose and fucoidan yields in Brown seaweeds (order Fucales) distributed along the coast of Urla (izmir, Turkey). J Aquac Fisheries. 2017;**1**:1-5

[84] Turan G, Tekogul H. The Turkish mezzes formulated with protein-rich green sea vegetable (chlorophyta), Ulva rigida, cultured in onshore tank system. Journal of Aquatic Food Products Technology. 2013;**23**(5):447-452. DOI: 10.1080/10498850.2012.723307

[85] Usov AI. Polysaccharides of the red algae. In: Derek H, editor. Advances in Carbohydrate Chemistry and Biochemistry, Vol. 65. London, UK: Academic Press; 2011. pp. 115-217

[86] Venkatesan J, Lowe B, Anil S, Manivasagan P, Kheraif AAA, Kang KH, 2015. Seaweed polysaccharides and their potential biomedical applications. Starch/Stärke, 67, 381-390

[87] Venugopal V. Marine Polysaccharides: Food Applications. Boca Raton, FL, USA: Taylor & Francis; 2016; 396 p

[88] Wang YZ, Zhang XH, Zhang JX. New insight into the kinetic behavior of the structural formation process in agar gelation. Rheologica Acta. 2013;**52**:39-48

[89] Whistler RL, BeMiller JN. Carbohydrate Chemistry for Food Scientists. St. Paul: Eagan Press; 1997; 241 p

[90] Yaich H, Garna H, Besbes S, Barthélemy JP, Paquot M, Blecker C. Impact of extraction procedures on the chemical, rheological and textural properties of ulvan from Ulva lactuca of Tunisia coast. Food Hydrocolloids. 2014;**40**:53-63

[91] Yamamoto M. Physicochemical studies on sulfated polysaccharides extracted from seaweeds at various temperatures. Agricultural and Biological Chemistry. 1980;**44**:589-593

Index